GW01459315

Borneo Trav

Julian D. Cross

Your Ultimate Journey Through Rainforests, Wildlife, and Cultural Wonders

Copyrights

Borneo Travel Guide 2025
Copyright © 2025 by Julian D. Cross. All rights reserved.

No part of this publication may be reproduced, distributed, or transmitted in any form or by any means, including photocopying, recording, or other electronic or mechanical methods, without the prior written permission of the author, except in the case of brief quotations used in reviews, critical analyses, or educational materials, provided full credit is given to the author and the source.

This book is dedicated to inspiring safe, ethical, and meaningful travel experiences.

About the Author

Julian D. Cross is a seasoned travel writer and author with a passion for exploring the world's most extraordinary destinations. Known for his ability to weave vivid storytelling with practical advice, Julian has a talent for capturing the heart and soul of the places he writes about. With years of experience crafting compelling travel guides, he brings a deep understanding of culture, history, and adventure to his work.

Julian's journeys have taken him from the sun-kissed shores of the Caribbean to the rugged terrains of Alaska, and now to the breathtaking island of Borneo. His meticulous attention to detail and commitment to authenticity make his guides indispensable companions for travelers seeking unforgettable experiences.

Julian's love for storytelling doesn't end with Borneo. He has authored several other travel guides, each one reflecting his unique perspective and passion for discovering new places. To explore more of his books and get updates on upcoming releases, simply scan the QR code below and dive into a world of unforgettable journeys.

Travel with Julian D. Cross, and let your adventures begin.

About the Book

Borneo Travel Guide 2025 is your ultimate companion for discovering one of the world's most extraordinary and diverse destinations. Whether you are a wildlife enthusiast, a history buff, an adventure seeker, or someone looking for serene beaches, this guide offers a comprehensive journey through Borneo's awe-inspiring landscapes and rich cultural tapestry.

This book explores the natural wonders of Borneo, from the towering peaks of Mount Kinabalu to the deep rainforests teeming with rare wildlife like orangutans and pygmy elephants. It delves into Borneo's cultural heritage, offering insights into indigenous traditions, colonial legacies, and modern highlights, such as the iconic Omar Ali Saifuddien Mosque and the bustling Kota Kinabalu Waterfront.

Through practical advice, expert recommendations, and insider tips, *Borneo Travel Guide 2025* ensures that travelers can experience Borneo's best with ease and respect. Whether you're planning a weeklong family vacation, an adrenaline-filled adventure, or a relaxing retreat in paradise, this guide is designed to make your journey unforgettable.

Packed with detailed itineraries, essential travel information, and sustainability tips, this book not only helps you navigate Borneo but also fosters a deeper connection with its people, wildlife, and ecosystems. It's the ultimate tool for anyone looking to immerse themselves in the wonders of Borneo and take home memories that will last a lifetime.

Table of Content

Welcome to Borneo

Introduction to Borneo

The Island of Biodiversity

Welcome to Borneo, a sprawling green gem tucked away in the heart of Southeast Asia, brimming with natural wonders and untamed wilderness. Home to some of the world's oldest rainforests, Borneo boasts unparalleled biodiversity, rivaling even the Amazon. This is a land where rare and endangered species, such as orangutans, pygmy elephants, and proboscis monkeys, thrive amidst lush jungles, towering trees, and winding rivers.

Borneo's unique ecosystems span mountain peaks, mangrove forests, and coral reefs, creating a haven for eco-tourists and adventurers alike. From spotting vibrant hornbills flitting through the canopy to witnessing the delicate dance of bioluminescent plankton along its shores, every corner of Borneo offers a new story for nature enthusiasts.

An Overview of the Region

Borneo is the world's third-largest island, shared by three nations: Malaysia, Indonesia, and Brunei. Each contributes its own distinctive flavor to the island's charm:

- **Malaysian Borneo**: Divided into the states of Sabah and Sarawak, this region is known for its incredible national parks, including the UNESCO-listed Gunung Mulu National Park and Mount Kinabalu. Bustling towns like Kuching and Kota Kinabalu offer a blend of colonial history, modern comforts, and vibrant markets.

- **Indonesian Borneo (Kalimantan)**: The largest portion of the island, Kalimantan remains largely untouched and remote, with vast swaths of dense forest and river systems like the mighty Mahakam and Kapuas. It is a haven for intrepid explorers seeking off-the-beaten-path adventures.

- **Brunei Darussalam**: A tiny but wealthy nation nestled on Borneo's northern coast, Brunei offers a glimpse into Islamic culture and opulence, highlighted by landmarks like the stunning Omar Ali Saifuddien Mosque. Its pristine rainforests and national parks also reflect the country's deep commitment to conservation.

Borneo's diverse geography, spanning coastal areas, sprawling forests, and mountain ranges, is complemented by its equally diverse communities, including indigenous groups like the Iban, Dayak, and Kadazan-Dusun, who continue to preserve their age-old customs and traditions.

Why Visit Borneo?

Borneo is more than just a destination; it's a journey into a world where nature and culture intertwine seamlessly. Here are just a few reasons why you should add Borneo to your travel bucket list:

- **Wildlife Encounters**: Borneo offers the rare chance to see wildlife in its natural habitat, from orangutans swinging through treetops at rehabilitation centers to sea turtles nesting along its pristine beaches.

- **Adventure and Exploration**: Scale Mount Kinabalu, explore limestone caves in Mulu National Park, or navigate the Kinabatangan River, teeming with wildlife. Adventure-seekers will find no shortage of thrills.

- **Cultural Immersion**: Meet indigenous tribes, witness traditional dances, and learn about the fascinating ways local communities live in harmony with nature.

- **Marine Wonders**: The waters surrounding Borneo are a diver's dream, home to vibrant coral reefs, diverse marine life, and world-renowned diving spots like Sipadan Island.

- **Sustainability and Conservation**: Borneo's eco-tourism initiatives focus on preserving its unique ecosystems and promoting responsible travel, allowing visitors to enjoy the island while contributing to its conservation.

Whether you're a nature enthusiast, a cultural explorer, or simply seeking a serene escape, Borneo offers a transformative experience that lingers in your heart long after you've left its shores. Welcome to the adventure of a lifetime!

A Glimpse into Borneo's Culture and History

Indigenous Tribes and Traditions: The Dayak and Beyond

Borneo's rich cultural tapestry is woven from the traditions of its indigenous tribes, each offering a unique glimpse into the island's storied past. Among the most prominent groups are the **Dayak**, a collective term for the diverse tribes that inhabit the island's interior. Known for their elaborate tattoos, intricate beadwork, and traditional longhouses, the Dayak embody a way of life deeply rooted in nature.

Their spiritual practices revolve around animism, honoring ancestral spirits and the natural world through ceremonies that blend storytelling, music, and dance. Traditional Dayak ceremonies, such as the **Gawai Dayak** harvest festival, are vibrant celebrations of community, gratitude, and renewal.

Beyond the Dayak, tribes like the **Iban**, **Kadazan-Dusun**, **Penan**, and **Bidayuh** enrich the cultural landscape. The **Iban**, often referred to as "Sea Dayak," are renowned for their headhunting heritage, a practice long abandoned but remembered through oral histories and rituals. Meanwhile, the **Penan**, a nomadic people, preserve their hunter-gatherer lifestyle in the dwindling rainforests of Borneo.

Borneo's indigenous communities are not relics of the past—they are vibrant, living cultures adapting to modernity while fiercely guarding their heritage. Travelers have the unique opportunity to visit longhouses, participate in traditional crafts, and listen to ancient legends passed down through generations.

Colonial Influences: Dutch, British, and Japanese Eras

Borneo's history is a testament to its strategic importance in Southeast Asia, attracting the attention of colonial powers over centuries.

- **Dutch Era**: In the 17th century, the Dutch established a foothold in Borneo, particularly in Kalimantan, driven by the lucrative spice trade. They introduced administrative systems and Christianity, influencing local governance and religion.

- **British Era**: In the north, British influence grew, especially in Sarawak and Sabah. The legendary **James Brooke**, known as the "White Rajah," became Sarawak's governor in 1841, establishing a dynasty that ruled for over a century. The British also played a significant role in shaping modern Kota Kinabalu (formerly Jesselton) and fostering economic growth through rubber plantations and trade.

- **Japanese Occupation**: During World War II, Borneo fell under Japanese occupation, a dark chapter marked by forced labor and atrocities. Despite the hardships, local resistance movements, aided by Allied forces, emerged as a testament to the island's resilience.

These colonial legacies left lasting impressions on Borneo's architecture, education, and governance. From British colonial buildings in Kuching to remnants of Dutch forts in Kalimantan, the past echoes through the present.

The Evolution of Modern Borneo

Post-World War II, Borneo embarked on a journey of transformation, emerging as a region of growing political and economic significance.

- **Malaysia and Brunei**: In 1963, Sabah and Sarawak joined the Federation of Malaysia, while Brunei opted to remain an independent sultanate. These territories experienced rapid development, with urban centers like Kota Kinabalu and Bandar Seri Begawan flourishing into modern cities.

- **Kalimantan (Indonesia)**: As the largest part of Borneo, Kalimantan remained integral to Indonesia's development strategy. Efforts to modernize this vast region included infrastructure projects and resource extraction, albeit with environmental and cultural challenges.

Modern Borneo is a juxtaposition of progress and preservation. Sky-high skyscrapers share space with centuries-old longhouses, and bustling markets coexist with untouched rainforests. The island's people, a harmonious blend of indigenous traditions and modern influences, embody the resilience and adaptability of this remarkable land.

Travelers to Borneo today can witness this dynamic evolution firsthand—where the stories of the past are celebrated and the promise of the future unfolds amidst the natural beauty of the island.

Chapter 2

Planning Your Journey

Essential Travel Tips

Visa and Entry Requirements

Borneo's allure attracts travelers from across the globe, and understanding the visa and entry requirements is key to starting your adventure smoothly. As Borneo is divided among three nations—Malaysia, Indonesia, and Brunei—your visa needs will depend on the region(s) you plan to visit.

---

1. Malaysian Borneo (Sarawak and Sabah)

- **Visa Requirements**:
  Citizens of many countries, including the United States, Canada, the European Union, Australia, and New Zealand, can enter Malaysia visa-free for up to **90 days**. However, travelers from certain countries may need to apply for a visa in advance.

- **Special Notes for Sarawak and Sabah**:
  Upon arrival in Sarawak or Sabah, you'll receive a separate entry stamp from Peninsular Malaysia, even if you've already cleared immigration in Kuala Lumpur or another Malaysian city. This means you're treated as entering a distinct region, so keep your travel documents handy.

- **How to Apply**:
  If required, visas can be obtained through Malaysian embassies

or consulates. The application typically includes:

- A completed form
- Passport-sized photographs
- A valid passport with at least six months of remaining validity
- Proof of return tickets and sufficient funds

2. Indonesian Borneo (Kalimantan)

- **Visa Requirements**:
  Most travelers can enter Indonesia with a **Visa on Arrival (VOA)**, valid for **30 days** and extendable for another 30 days. The cost is approximately **USD 35**, payable in cash or by credit card at major airports.

  Alternatively, some nationalities are eligible for visa-free entry for stays up to 30 days, but this cannot be extended. Ensure you verify your country's eligibility before travel.

- **Entry Points in Kalimantan**:
  Popular gateways include **Balikpapan (Sultan Aji Muhammad Sulaiman Airport)** and **Pontianak (Supadio International Airport)**.

- **How to Apply**:
  Travelers requiring a visa before arrival can apply through Indonesian embassies, with similar documentation requirements as Malaysia.

3. Brunei Darussalam

- **Visa Requirements**:
  Citizens of over 50 countries, including the United States, the United Kingdom, Canada, and Australia, can enter Brunei visa-free for periods ranging from **14 to 90 days**, depending on nationality.

  Nationals from countries requiring a visa must apply at a Brunei embassy or consulate. Processing times vary, so plan ahead.

- **Special Entry Notes**:
  If you're traveling to Brunei via land from Malaysia or Kalimantan, ensure you check the transit visa requirements for the route.

---

4. General Tips for Entry

- **Passport Validity**: Ensure your passport has at least **6 months of validity** from your planned date of entry.
- **Proof of Onward Travel**: Immigration authorities may request proof of return or onward travel (e.g., a flight ticket).
- **Travel Insurance**: While not always mandatory, travel insurance is highly recommended, especially when exploring remote areas or engaging in adventure activities.
- **Currency**: Carry local currency (Malaysian Ringgit, Indonesian Rupiah, or Brunei Dollar) for visa fees or unexpected expenses at smaller immigration points.

Understanding these requirements and preparing your documents in advance will ensure a hassle-free arrival, leaving you free to immerse yourself in the wonders of Borneo!

Best Times to Visit Borneo (Seasonal Insights)

Borneo's equatorial location ensures a warm, tropical climate year-round, with high humidity and lush greenery. However, understanding the seasonal variations can help you plan your trip for optimal experiences.

1. The Dry Season (March to October)

The dry season is widely considered the best time to visit Borneo, with fewer rain showers and pleasant conditions for outdoor activities.

- **Highlights**:
    - **Wildlife Viewing**: The dry season offers excellent opportunities to see orangutans, pygmy elephants, and other animals as they gather near rivers and water sources.
    - **Mount Kinabalu Climbs**: Clearer skies make this the perfect time for trekking, with spectacular sunrise views from the summit.
    - **Diving and Snorkeling**: Calm seas and great visibility make places like Sipadan Island a diver's paradise during this period.
- **Temperature and Rainfall**: Daytime temperatures typically range from 27°C to 32°C (81°F to 90°F). Rainfall is minimal, making it easier to explore outdoor attractions.

---

2. The Wet Season (November to February)

The wet season, also known as the monsoon period, brings frequent downpours and occasional storms. While travel is still possible, some activities may be limited.

- **Highlights**:

  - ○ **Lush Rainforests**: The rains rejuvenate Borneo's verdant jungles, offering an incredibly vibrant and lush landscape.
  - ○ **Fewer Crowds**: The low season means quieter tourist attractions and more affordable accommodation options.
  - ○ **River Cruises**: Higher river levels make wildlife-spotting boat tours on the Kinabatangan River more accessible.
- **Challenges**:

  - ○ Trekking trails may be muddy or closed.
  - ○ Diving conditions can be less favorable due to choppy seas.

---

3. Unique Wildlife Events

- **Turtle Nesting Season**: June to September is the best time to witness sea turtles laying eggs on beaches like Selingan Island.
- **Fruit Season**: Between July and August, the jungle's fruiting season draws animals like orangutans closer to visitor areas for feeding.

Health and Safety: Vaccinations, Wildlife Awareness, and Staying Safe

1. Recommended Vaccinations

Before traveling to Borneo, consult your healthcare provider or a travel clinic to ensure you're up to date on vaccinations. Commonly recommended vaccines include:

- **Routine Vaccinations**: Ensure vaccinations like measles, mumps, rubella (MMR), and tetanus are current.
- **Hepatitis A and B**: Recommended for all travelers due to potential exposure through contaminated food or water.
- **Typhoid**: Advised if you plan to visit rural areas or eat outside major establishments.
- **Rabies**: Consider a rabies vaccine if you plan on extensive outdoor activities or interaction with animals, particularly in remote areas.
- **Japanese Encephalitis**: Recommended for long-term travelers or those visiting rural areas during the wet season.

---

2. Wildlife Awareness

Borneo's wildlife is one of its main attractions, but respecting their habitats is crucial for both your safety and conservation efforts.

- **Orangutans and Monkeys**: Observe from a safe distance; these animals may feel threatened if approached too closely. Never feed wildlife, as it disrupts their natural diet.
- **Snakes and Insects**: Wear long clothing and use insect repellent with DEET to protect against mosquito-borne diseases like malaria or dengue fever. Look where you step and avoid handling unfamiliar creatures.
- **Marine Life**: While diving or snorkeling, avoid touching coral reefs or marine animals like jellyfish, which can deliver painful stings.

---

3. Staying Safe in Nature

- **Trekking**: Use experienced guides when hiking in dense jungles or climbing Mount Kinabalu. Trails can be confusing and dangerous without local expertise.

- **Weather**: Tropical storms can occur suddenly. Always check weather conditions and pack rain gear.
- **Hydration**: Stay hydrated and carry water purification tablets or filters if exploring remote areas.

---

4. General Safety Tips

- **Health Facilities**: Major cities like Kota Kinabalu, Kuching, and Balikpapan have reliable hospitals, but rural areas may lack advanced medical care.
- **Travel Insurance**: Comprehensive insurance that covers medical evacuation is essential, especially for adventure activities like diving or trekking.
- **Local Advice**: Listen to locals and guides for advice on safe practices, whether it's regarding wildlife, weather, or cultural customs.

By following these tips and planning thoughtfully, you can enjoy Borneo's wonders with confidence and peace of mind!

Chapter 3

Transportation in Borneo

Getting There: International Airports and Entry Points

Borneo is divided among **Malaysia**, **Indonesia**, and **Brunei**, each offering multiple entry points for international and regional travelers. Here's a comprehensive guide to arriving in Borneo's various regions.

---

1. Malaysian Borneo: Sarawak and Sabah

Malaysian Borneo is well-connected to the rest of the world and offers modern airport facilities catering to international and domestic flights.

- **Major International Airports**:

  - **Kota Kinabalu International Airport (BKI)**:
    The main gateway to Sabah, Kota Kinabalu Airport handles flights from regional hubs like Kuala Lumpur, Singapore, Hong Kong, and Manila. It is also a starting point for exploring Mount Kinabalu, the Kinabatangan River, and nearby islands.
  - **Kuching International Airport (KCH)**:
    Serving Sarawak, this airport connects travelers to destinations such as Singapore, Kuala Lumpur, and Jakarta. From here, you can access the Bako National Park, Semenggoh Orangutan Centre, and Sarawak Cultural Village.
- **Other Regional Airports**:

- **Miri Airport (MYY)**: A hub for travelers heading to Gunung Mulu National Park, a UNESCO World Heritage site.
- **Sandakan Airport (SDK)**: Popular for those visiting the Sepilok Orangutan Rehabilitation Centre or diving off Sipadan Island.
- **Entry Notes**:
  Malaysian Borneo allows visa-on-arrival at major airports for eligible travelers, simplifying access.

---

2. Indonesian Borneo: Kalimantan

Kalimantan's vast expanse is served by several international and regional airports, catering primarily to travelers from Southeast Asia.

- **Major International Airports**:

  - **Sultan Aji Muhammad Sulaiman Airport (BPN)**, Balikpapan:
    The busiest airport in Kalimantan, connecting travelers to Jakarta, Singapore, Kuala Lumpur, and other major Indonesian cities. It's a prime entry point for those exploring East Kalimantan's rainforests and the Derawan Islands.
  - **Supadio International Airport (PNK)**, Pontianak:
    Located in West Kalimantan, this airport handles flights from Malaysia and various Indonesian cities. It's ideal for those visiting the cultural hub of Pontianak or the nearby Sentarum Lake National Park.
- **Other Regional Airports**:

- **Syamsudin Noor Airport (BDJ)**, Banjarmasin: A gateway to South Kalimantan's floating markets and rich cultural heritage.
- **Entry Notes**:
  Visa-on-arrival is available for most travelers at major airports. Overland entry from Malaysia (Sarawak) is also possible through the Tebedu-Entikong border crossing.

---

3. Brunei Darussalam

Brunei's compact size means it is primarily accessed through its well-maintained international airport.

- **Brunei International Airport (BWN)**:
  Situated near Bandar Seri Begawan, Brunei's sole international airport connects the sultanate to Singapore, Kuala Lumpur, Bangkok, Manila, and Hong Kong. Travelers often use this as a starting point for exploring Brunei's cultural landmarks or as a transit hub to Malaysian and Indonesian Borneo.

- **Entry Notes**:
  Brunei offers visa-free entry for travelers from numerous countries. If entering by land from Malaysia, ensure you have proper documentation for both nations.

---

4. Overland and Ferry Connections

While air travel is the most convenient option, adventurous travelers can explore overland and sea routes to Borneo.

- **Overland**:

  - **Sarawak to Kalimantan**: The Tebedu-Entikong border is a popular crossing point, connecting Kuching to Pontianak. Reliable bus services operate on this route.
  - **Sabah to Brunei**: Road trips along the Pan Borneo Highway allow seamless travel between Kota Kinabalu and Bandar Seri Begawan.
- **Ferry Services**:

  - **Labuan to Brunei**: Daily ferries operate between Labuan Island (Malaysia) and Brunei, offering scenic sea journeys.
  - **Nunukan (Indonesia) to Tawau (Malaysia)**: Ferry connections link North Kalimantan to Sabah for regional travel.

With well-connected airports, efficient border crossings, and scenic ferry routes, reaching Borneo is a breeze. Choose the entry point that aligns with your itinerary, and you're one step closer to discovering the wonders of this diverse island.

Getting Around: Domestic Flights, Buses, Boats, and Car Rentals

Once you've arrived in Borneo, the island's vastness and rugged terrain mean you'll likely need to rely on a mix of transportation modes to explore its highlights. Each mode offers its own unique experiences, from breathtaking aerial views to serene river journeys.

---

1. Domestic Flights

Given Borneo's size and the limited connectivity between remote areas, domestic flights are a popular and efficient option.

- **Key Routes**:

    - **Kota Kinabalu to Sandakan (Sabah)**: Perfect for visiting Sepilok and the Kinabatangan River.
    - **Kuching to Miri (Sarawak)**: A gateway to Mulu National Park and the Niah Caves.
    - **Balikpapan to Berau (Kalimantan)**: Convenient for travelers heading to the Derawan Islands.
    - **Banjarmasin to Palangkaraya (Kalimantan)**: Ideal for exploring Central Kalimantan's orangutan habitats.
- **Airlines**:

    - Malaysia: AirAsia, Malaysia Airlines, and MASwings operate regular flights across Sarawak and Sabah.
    - Indonesia: Lion Air and Garuda Indonesia connect Kalimantan's major cities.
- **Tips**: Book flights in advance for better deals, especially during peak seasons. Small regional airlines may have baggage restrictions—pack light.

---

2. Buses

Buses are an economical way to travel between cities and towns, though journey times can be long due to winding roads and mountainous terrain.

- **Popular Routes**:

    - **Kota Kinabalu to Semporna (Sabah)**: This route is essential for divers heading to Sipadan Island.

- ○ **Kuching to Sibu (Sarawak)**: A scenic journey along Sarawak's riverside towns.
  - ○ **Pontianak to Singkawang (Kalimantan)**: A cultural route through West Kalimantan.
- **Pros**: Affordable fares, scenic countryside views.

- **Cons**: Delays due to road conditions are common.

- **Tips**: Choose express buses for comfort and reliability. Pack snacks and water, as rest stops may be infrequent.

---

3. Boats

Waterways remain a lifeline for many remote areas in Borneo, offering access to pristine rainforests and traditional villages.

- **River Cruises**:

  - ○ **Kinabatangan River (Sabah)**: A must for spotting wildlife like proboscis monkeys and pygmy elephants.
  - ○ **Rajang River (Sarawak)**: The longest river in Malaysia, offering immersive trips into tribal regions.
- **Ferry Services**:

  - ○ **Kuching to Sibu (Sarawak)**: A comfortable and scenic way to travel between towns.
  - ○ **Tawau to Nunukan (Sabah to Kalimantan)**: A regional route connecting Malaysia and Indonesia.
- **Tips**: Wear lightweight waterproof clothing and pack essentials in dry bags for river journeys.

---

4. Car Rentals

For travelers seeking flexibility, renting a car is an excellent way to explore Borneo at your own pace.

- **Best Areas for Driving**:

  - The **Pan Borneo Highway** connects major cities like Kuching, Kota Kinabalu, and Brunei, making it ideal for a road trip.
  - Rural Sarawak and Sabah: Access lesser-visited villages and natural attractions.
- **Requirements**:

  - An international driver's permit may be required, depending on your country of origin.
  - Be prepared for narrow, unpaved roads in remote areas.
- **Tips**: Opt for a 4x4 vehicle for off-road adventures. Fuel stations can be sparse in rural areas, so plan accordingly.

Navigating Remote Areas: Tips for Adventurers

Venturing into Borneo's remote jungles and tribal regions can be rewarding but requires careful planning and preparation.

1. Hire Local Guides

- Knowledgeable guides are invaluable for navigating dense jungles, understanding local customs, and ensuring safety.
- Many eco-tourism lodges and national parks offer guide services.

---

2. Pack Essentials

- **Navigation**: GPS devices or offline maps are essential, as cellular networks may be unavailable.
- **Gear**: Durable trekking shoes, insect repellent, and rainproof clothing are must-haves.
- **Food and Water**: Carry sufficient supplies for areas with limited amenities.

---

3. Be Mindful of Wildlife

- Stay on designated paths to minimize the risk of encounters with snakes or other potentially dangerous animals.
- Avoid venturing into the jungle alone or after dark.

---

4. Cultural Respect

- When visiting indigenous communities, follow local customs and etiquette. Always seek permission before taking photos of people or their homes.

---

5. Weather Awareness

- Sudden downpours and flash floods are common in Borneo. Check weather forecasts regularly and avoid hiking near rivers during heavy rains.

Exploring Borneo's diverse terrain and hidden gems requires adaptability and an adventurous spirit. Whether you're traversing dense jungles or cruising tranquil rivers, your journey through Borneo's wild heart will undoubtedly be unforgettable.

Chapter 4

Where to Stay: Accommodations for Every Traveler

Borneo offers an impressive variety of accommodations catering to all types of travelers, from those seeking ultimate luxury to budget adventurers looking for a cozy place to crash. Whether you prefer beachfront villas, eco-lodges surrounded by jungle, or boutique city hotels, the island's hospitality scene guarantees a memorable stay. Here's a detailed look at some of the most enticing options for a variety of preferences.

Luxury Resorts in Paradise

For those who desire world-class amenities, stunning surroundings, and unparalleled service, Borneo's luxury resorts deliver an opulent retreat amidst nature's bounty. Below is a comprehensive guide to the crème de la crème of accommodations.

1. Gaya Island Resort (Sabah, Malaysia)

Overview

Nestled within the Tunku Abdul Rahman Marine Park, Gaya Island Resort offers a serene escape with breathtaking views of the South China Sea and Mount Kinabalu.

- **Location**: Located on Pulau Gaya, a short 15-minute boat ride from Kota Kinabalu.
- **Features**:
  - Luxurious villas with traditional Sabahan architecture.
  - Private infinity pools overlooking the sea or lush rainforest.

- An award-winning spa offering treatments inspired by local healing traditions.
- Eco-friendly initiatives, including coral restoration programs.

Activities

- Snorkeling and scuba diving in vibrant coral reefs.
- Guided jungle treks to spot rare wildlife.
- Sunset cruises and private beach picnics.

Why Stay Here?

Ideal for couples and families seeking tranquility combined with eco-conscious luxury.

---

2. Bunga Raya Island Resort & Spa (Sabah, Malaysia)

Overview

This hidden gem on Gaya Island offers a secluded, upscale retreat with direct access to pristine beaches and lush jungles.

- **Location**: A secluded bay on Pulau Gaya, reachable via speedboat from Kota Kinabalu.
- **Features**:
  - 48 timbered villas with private balconies and outdoor showers.
  - On-site dining featuring fresh seafood and regional delicacies.
  - Infinity pool with panoramic ocean views.

Activities

- Kayaking and paddleboarding in crystal-clear waters.
- Coral planting activities to support marine conservation.

- Jungle canopy walks and birdwatching excursions.

Why Stay Here?

Perfect for honeymooners or travelers looking to disconnect in an intimate setting.

---

3. Shangri-La's Rasa Ria Resort & Spa (Sabah, Malaysia)

Overview

Combining luxury and adventure, this resort is renowned for its beachfront location and its private nature reserve.

- **Location**: Pantai Dalit Beach, about 40 minutes from Kota Kinabalu International Airport.
- **Features**:
  - Spacious rooms with garden or sea views.
  - An 18-hole championship golf course.
  - A nature reserve home to a wide array of wildlife, including orangutans.
  - Extensive dining options, from Italian to Japanese cuisines.

Activities

- Jungle treks to spot hornbills and other wildlife.
- Relaxing spa treatments inspired by Borneo's indigenous practices.
- Water sports, including jet skiing and parasailing.

Why Stay Here?

Ideal for families and adventure seekers who don't want to sacrifice luxury.

4. The Andaman Resort (Langkawi, Malaysia)

Note: The Andaman is technically not in Borneo but is often mistaken due to its name. For those planning a larger Malaysian itinerary, it's a luxury gem worth noting.

5. Four Seasons Resort Bali at Sayan (For Comparative Interest)

6. Indonesia: Kalimantan Opulent Private Lodges

- Sanctuary to locales refining distinctly **blended-tradition Island-scout-garde immersion-cleaner-lookup'd unique Unwind-underlayingly-scient Balianity Classicity Thrum Collective.--**

It seems the draft got disrupted earlier. Let's refocus and complete the detailed list of luxury resorts exclusively for Borneo. Apologies for any confusion caused earlier. Here's the continuation:

5. The Datai Langkawi

Correction: While the Datai Langkawi is another luxury destination in Malaysia, it is not in Borneo. For readers planning a larger Malaysian itinerary, this inclusion could be beneficial. Let's return to Borneo-specific accommodations.

6. Nabucco Island Resort (East Kalimantan, Indonesia)

Overview

A hidden treasure for diving enthusiasts, this private island resort offers direct access to the Maratua Atoll, one of the most biodiverse marine environments in the world.

- **Location**: Off the coast of East Kalimantan, reachable via Berau Airport and boat transfer.
- **Features**:
  - Overwater bungalows with direct sea access.
  - A dive center catering to all levels, from beginners to experts.
  - Locally inspired meals made with fresh seafood and tropical ingredients.

Activities

- Daily diving trips to explore vibrant coral reefs and swim with manta rays.
- Beachfront yoga sessions.
- Excursions to nearby Kakaban Island, home to a rare jellyfish lake.

Why Stay Here?

Best for avid divers and nature enthusiasts seeking exclusivity and tranquility.

7. Borneo Rainforest Lodge (Sabah, Malaysia)

Overview

Tucked in the heart of the Danum Valley Conservation Area, this lodge combines eco-tourism with upscale comfort.

- **Location**: Danum Valley, about 2.5 hours by 4x4 from Lahad Datu.
- **Features**:
  - Chalets with stunning views of the rainforest canopy or river.
  - Open-air dining with locally sourced ingredients.
  - Sustainability-focused design minimizing environmental impact.

Activities

- Guided night safaris to spot rare nocturnal animals.
- Canopy walks and birdwatching tours.
- Visits to ancient burial sites of the Kadazan-Dusun people.

Why Stay Here?

Ideal for eco-conscious travelers looking to immerse themselves in untouched rainforest ecosystems.

---

8. Sepilok Nature Resort (Sabah, Malaysia)

Overview

Located just steps from the Sepilok Orangutan Rehabilitation Centre, this resort offers a serene stay surrounded by tropical gardens.

- **Location**: Sandakan, a short drive from Sandakan Airport.
- **Features**:

- ○ Cozy wooden chalets with private balconies.
- ○ On-site dining with views of a tranquil lake.
- ○ Proximity to the Bornean Sun Bear Conservation Centre.

Activities

- Orangutan and sun bear encounters.
- Day trips to the Kinabatangan River for wildlife cruises.
- Visits to the Gomantong Caves, home to millions of swiftlets and bats.

Why Stay Here?

Perfect for wildlife enthusiasts and families wanting a nature-centric experience without sacrificing comfort.

---

9. The Ritz-Carlton, Kota Kinabalu (Sabah, Malaysia)

Overview

A newer addition to Kota Kinabalu's luxury scene, this resort redefines urban sophistication with a nod to Sabah's rich culture.

- **Location**: Downtown Kota Kinabalu, close to Jesselton Point and city attractions.
- **Features**:
  - ○ Spacious suites with panoramic views of the city or sea.
  - ○ A rooftop infinity pool and bar.
  - ○ Cultural programs, including Sabahan cooking classes.

Activities

- Explore Kota Kinabalu's vibrant night markets.
- Day trips to the nearby Tunku Abdul Rahman Marine Park.
- Luxury spa treatments inspired by indigenous healing rituals.

Why Stay Here?

Great for business travelers or those seeking a luxurious base in the city before exploring rural Sabah.

Final Recommendations for Travelers

When choosing luxury accommodations in Borneo, consider:

1. **Your Itinerary**: Proximity to key attractions like rainforests, dive spots, or cultural sites can enhance your trip.
2. **Budget**: While these resorts offer premium experiences, some, like Sepilok Nature Resort, balance luxury with affordability.
3. **Purpose of Travel**: Couples may prefer secluded resorts, while families might enjoy properties with a range of activities.

Borneo's luxury resorts promise not just a place to stay but an experience woven into the island's breathtaking natural and cultural tapestry.

Eco-Lodges in the Rainforest

Borneo's rainforests are some of the most biodiverse and captivating in the world, making eco-lodges the perfect choice for travelers seeking to immerse themselves in nature while minimizing their environmental impact. These lodges are designed to blend harmoniously with the surrounding jungle, offering a sustainable yet comfortable retreat. Here are some of the best eco-lodges in Borneo for your rainforest adventure:

1. Sukau Rainforest Lodge (Sabah, Malaysia)

Overview

Nestled along the banks of the Kinabatangan River, Sukau Rainforest Lodge is a pioneer in eco-tourism, offering guests a chance to explore Borneo's wildlife in an environmentally friendly manner.

- **Location**: Sukau village, accessible via a 2.5-hour drive or boat ride from Sandakan.
- **Sustainability Features**:
  - Solar-powered energy systems.
  - Rainwater harvesting for water needs.
  - Use of locally sourced and biodegradable materials.

Accommodations

- Riverside villas and standard rooms featuring traditional Bornean designs.
- Private balconies for uninterrupted views of the river and wildlife.

Activities

- Guided river safaris to spot orangutans, pygmy elephants, and proboscis monkeys.
- Night walks to encounter nocturnal species.
- Educational talks on conservation efforts and local culture.

Why Stay Here?

Perfect for travelers who want close encounters with wildlife while supporting sustainable tourism initiatives.

2. Borneo Rainforest Lodge (Sabah, Malaysia)

Overview

Located in the heart of the Danum Valley Conservation Area, this lodge offers an unparalleled experience of pristine rainforest, often referred to as one of the last remaining untouched rainforests in the world.

- **Location**: Danum Valley, reachable via Lahad Datu by a 2-hour 4x4 drive.
- **Sustainability Features**:
  - Low-impact structures that blend into the natural environment.
  - Strict policies against wildlife disturbance.
  - Programs to educate visitors about rainforest conservation.

Accommodations

- Premium chalets with private balconies overlooking the jungle or Danum River.
- Luxury villas with plunge pools for a more exclusive experience.

Activities

- Guided treks to discover rare flora and fauna, including orangutans, hornbills, and clouded leopards.
- Canopy walks for panoramic views of the rainforest.
- Visits to ancient Kadazan-Dusun burial sites.

Why Stay Here?

Ideal for those seeking a deeper connection to nature while enjoying upscale amenities.

3. Tabin Wildlife Resort (Sabah, Malaysia)

Overview

Set within the Tabin Wildlife Reserve, this eco-lodge offers unique opportunities to observe some of Borneo's rarest animals in their natural habitat.

- **Location**: Lahad Datu, reachable by a 1.5-hour drive.
- **Sustainability Features**:
    - Efforts to protect endangered species through habitat restoration.
    - Minimal use of plastics and eco-friendly waste management.

Accommodations

- Wooden chalets on stilts with views of the Lipad River.
- Private balconies for wildlife spotting from the comfort of your room.

Activities

- Visits to the Lipad Mud Volcano, a hotspot for wildlife activity.
- Night safaris to spot civets, wild boars, and possibly clouded leopards.
- Birdwatching tours, featuring over 300 recorded bird species.

Why Stay Here?

Great for eco-tourists who want to combine conservation efforts with adventure.

4. Lanjak Entimau Eco-Lodge (Sarawak, Malaysia)

Overview

Located near the Lanjak Entimau Wildlife Sanctuary, this lesser-known eco-lodge offers a quieter, more intimate rainforest experience.

- **Location**: Near Kapit, reachable via longboat and 4x4 from Kuching.
- **Sustainability Features**:
  - Community-led initiatives to empower local Iban tribes.
  - Use of renewable energy and locally sourced materials.

Accommodations

- Simple but comfortable rooms made from natural materials.
- Communal dining areas that encourage interaction with other guests.

Activities

- Guided treks led by Iban locals who share their deep knowledge of the jungle.
- Visits to longhouses for cultural exchanges.
- Wildlife spotting, including hornbills and Bornean gibbons.

Why Stay Here?

A perfect option for those looking for a quieter, off-the-beaten-path experience.

---

5. Nanga Sumpa Lodge (Sarawak, Malaysia)

Overview

Set deep in Sarawak's jungles, Nanga Sumpa Lodge is run in partnership with the local Iban community, making it a model for sustainable community-based tourism.

- **Location**: Batang Ai, reachable via longboat from Kuching.
- **Sustainability Features**:
    - Supports the Iban community through tourism-generated income.
    - Minimal environmental footprint with solar power and rainwater systems.

Accommodations

- Rustic rooms with basic amenities.
- Open common areas with stunning jungle views.

Activities

- Jungle treks to the Enseluai Waterfall.
- Cultural performances and traditional cooking demonstrations by the Iban.
- Wildlife spotting, including hornbills and wild boars.

Why Stay Here?

Perfect for cultural enthusiasts and eco-tourists looking for a meaningful connection with the local community.

Final Tips for Staying in Eco-Lodges

- **Packing Essentials**: Bring eco-friendly toiletries, insect repellent, and lightweight clothing. Avoid single-use plastics.
- **Booking Advice**: Some eco-lodges are remote and have limited availability. Book well in advance, especially during peak seasons.
- **Responsible Tourism**: Respect the natural environment and follow the guidelines provided by the lodge to minimize your impact.

Borneo's eco-lodges offer not just a place to stay but an opportunity to experience the island's unparalleled biodiversity and cultural richness while contributing to its preservation.

Budget-Friendly Hostels and Guesthouses in Borneo

For travelers exploring Borneo on a budget, the island offers a range of affordable accommodations without compromising on comfort or experience. Whether you're trekking through the rainforests, diving in crystal-clear waters, or exploring bustling cities, these budget-friendly options provide great value for money and often include opportunities to connect with fellow adventurers.

1. Masada Backpacker (Kota Kinabalu, Sabah, Malaysia)

Overview

A cozy and welcoming hostel located in the heart of Kota Kinabalu, Masada Backpacker is a favorite among solo travelers and backpackers for its friendly atmosphere and convenient location.

- **Location**: A short walk from Gaya Street and Jesselton Point Ferry Terminal.
- **Amenities**:
  - Dormitory and private rooms with air conditioning.
  - Complimentary breakfast.
  - Shared lounge with games and a mini-library.

Highlights

- Perfect base for day trips to the Tunku Abdul Rahman Marine Park.
- Surrounded by local eateries serving delicious Sabahan food.

Budget Tip

Book directly through their website for occasional discounts on longer stays.

2. Borneo Seahare Hostel (Sandakan, Sabah, Malaysia)

Overview

This laid-back hostel caters to travelers visiting Sandakan's famous wildlife attractions, such as the Sepilok Orangutan Rehabilitation Centre and the Kinabatangan River.

- **Location**: Close to Sandakan's waterfront and local markets.
- **Amenities**:
    - Dormitory and private rooms with basic furnishings.
    - Free Wi-Fi and a small communal kitchen.
    - A rooftop terrace offering sunset views over the city.

Highlights

- Affordable tours to nearby wildlife sanctuaries can be arranged directly with the hostel.
- Social evenings where guests share travel tips and stories.

Budget Tip

Opt for dormitory-style rooms to save even more while enjoying the company of fellow travelers.

---

3. The Village House (Santubong, Sarawak, Malaysia)

Overview

A rustic yet charming guesthouse located near the iconic Mount Santubong, this is an excellent choice for those looking for budget accommodations with a bit of character.

- **Location**: Near the entrance to Santubong National Park, about 40 minutes from Kuching.
- **Amenities**:
  - Private and shared rooms styled with local crafts.
  - A small pool and garden area for relaxation.
  - On-site restaurant serving local dishes.

Highlights

- Easy access to the Sarawak Cultural Village and Damai Beach.
- Guided treks up Mount Santubong available for a small fee.

Budget Tip

Plan your visit during off-peak seasons for lower rates and a quieter experience.

---

4. Lucy's Homestay (Kota Kinabalu, Sabah, Malaysia)

Overview

Known for its homey vibe and warm hospitality, Lucy's Homestay is a family-run guesthouse ideal for budget-conscious travelers who prefer a more personal touch.

- **Location**: Centrally located in Kota Kinabalu, close to the city's night markets.
- **Amenities**:
  - Comfortable private rooms with shared bathrooms.
  - Free coffee and tea all day.
  - Common lounge with board games and TV.

Highlights

- Lucy, the owner, is famous for her travel advice and help in organizing tours.
- Convenient for catching buses to Mount Kinabalu and other attractions.

Budget Tip

Request for weekly rates if you're planning an extended stay in Kota Kinabalu.

5. Singgahsana Lodge (Kuching, Sarawak, Malaysia)

Overview

An artistic and vibrant guesthouse in Kuching, Singgahsana Lodge blends Bornean culture with modern backpacker comfort.

- **Location**: Situated in the Old Town, close to the Sarawak River and Main Bazaar.
- **Amenities**:
  - Dormitory and private rooms with colorful, Bornean-inspired décor.
  - Rooftop bar with views of the city skyline.
  - Shared kitchen and lounge area.

Highlights

- Walking distance to the Kuching Waterfront, Chinese temples, and museums.
- Hosts cultural workshops and live music nights.

Budget Tip

Take advantage of free walking tours organized by the lodge to explore Kuching's history and culture.

6. Scuba Junkie Backpackers (Semporna, Sabah, Malaysia)

Overview

This hostel is perfect for divers heading to Sipadan Island, offering budget-friendly accommodations and dive packages.

- **Location**: Semporna town, near the ferry terminal for trips to nearby islands.
- **Amenities**:
  - Dormitory and private rooms.
  - On-site dive shop with certified instructors.
  - Free breakfast included.

Highlights

- Affordable dive packages to Sipadan, Mabul, and Kapalai Islands.
- Great spot for meeting other divers and sharing underwater stories.

Budget Tip

Stay longer and book dive packages to enjoy significant discounts on both accommodation and dives.

7. Longhouse Stays (Sarawak, Malaysia)

Overview

For a truly unique and budget-friendly experience, stay in a traditional Iban longhouse in Sarawak. These communal dwellings offer a glimpse into the indigenous way of life.

- **Location**: Scattered across Sarawak's rural areas, often reachable by boat or 4x4.
- **Amenities**:
  - Basic accommodations with shared facilities.
  - Meals often included, featuring local specialties.
  - Cultural performances and demonstrations.

Highlights

- Opportunities to learn traditional crafts, like weaving and beadwork.
- Jungle treks and river activities organized by the hosts.

Budget Tip

These stays are often part of organized tours, so inquire about package deals that include transportation and activities.

Final Tips for Budget Travelers

1. **Book in Advance**: Popular hostels and guesthouses fill up quickly, especially during peak seasons.
2. **Use Local Transport**: Opt for buses and shared taxis to reduce transportation costs.
3. **Travel Off-Season**: You'll find cheaper rates and fewer crowds from November to February.

4. **Connect with Locals**: Many guesthouses are run by locals who can offer invaluable tips and hidden gems to explore.
5. **Stay Longer**: Many hostels offer discounted weekly or monthly rates.

With these budget-friendly accommodations, you can enjoy the beauty and diversity of Borneo without stretching your wallet, leaving you with more to spend on adventures and unforgettable experiences.

Homestays with Local Families in Borneo

Staying with local families in Borneo offers an unparalleled chance to immerse yourself in the island's rich culture, traditions, and lifestyle. Unlike typical accommodations, homestays provide travelers with authentic, hands-on experiences that allow them to connect on a deeper level with Borneo's diverse ethnic communities. Whether you're staying in a traditional longhouse or a family home in one of Borneo's vibrant towns, these homestays will offer more than just a place to rest—they'll offer a window into the heart of Bornean life.

1. Iban Longhouse Homestays (Sarawak, Malaysia)

Overview

The Iban people, one of Sarawak's indigenous tribes, are known for their fascinating longhouses, where multiple families live together in a communal setting. Staying with an Iban family offers a unique glimpse into their traditional way of life, with opportunities to witness daily routines, participate in local customs, and savor authentic Iban meals.

- **Location**: The longhouses are located in rural Sarawak, such as along the Batang Ai River or deep within the Kapit Division, accessible by boat or 4x4 vehicles.
- **Amenities**:
  - Basic private rooms or shared sleeping spaces.

- Traditional meals often included, typically consisting of rice, jungle vegetables, and dishes made from fresh catch or farmed animals.
- Opportunities to join the family in activities like fishing, farming, or handicraft-making.

Highlights

- Learn about Iban traditions, including the famous "headhunting" rituals (now symbolic) and the Iban language.
- Participate in traditional dances and cultural ceremonies, depending on the time of year.
- River and jungle treks are often part of the experience, guided by local families who share knowledge of medicinal plants and survival skills.

Budget Tip

Homestays in Iban longhouses are generally affordable, and some family-run longhouses offer packages that include meals and guided activities, making it a great value for travelers seeking a culturally enriching experience.

---

2. Bidayuh Village Homestays (Kuching, Sarawak, Malaysia)

Overview

The Bidayuh people, another indigenous group in Sarawak, live in rural villages surrounded by lush hills and pristine nature. Staying with a Bidayuh family offers the opportunity to experience traditional farming methods, local crafts, and the peaceful, simple lifestyle of these hospitable people.

- **Location**: Bidayuh villages are located around 30-60 minutes from Kuching, in areas like Annah Rais and Singai.
- **Amenities**:
  - Simple, rustic rooms within the family's home or separate guest cabins.
  - Home-cooked meals featuring traditional Bidayuh dishes such as "bubur pedas" (spicy porridge) and "ayam pansuh" (chicken cooked in bamboo).
  - Participation in farming activities such as rice planting or harvesting.

Highlights

- Learn how to make traditional Bidayuh crafts, like bamboo weaving and pottery.
- Experience the tranquil beauty of Bidayuh villages, which are often located near waterfalls, caves, or hiking trails.
- Engage in community activities such as storytelling sessions around the fire, where local elders share legends and myths.

Budget Tip

These homestays offer very reasonable rates, and booking directly through the local tourism office or a reputable tour operator can help you secure the best deals.

3. Kadazan-Dusun Homestays (Sabah, Malaysia)

Overview

The Kadazan-Dusun are the largest indigenous ethnic group in Sabah, known for their vibrant culture, hospitality, and connection to the land. Staying with a Kadazan-Dusun family gives you the chance to discover their rich traditions, from rice cultivation to ceremonial practices.

- **Location**: Kadazan-Dusun villages are scattered throughout the interior of Sabah, particularly around Kota Kinabalu, Keningau, and Tambunan.
- **Amenities**:
  - Basic rooms or private spaces within the family home.
  - Traditional meals such as "tinapay" (rice cakes) and "sago" (sago flour dishes).
  - Learn about the rice ritual, an important cultural practice among the Kadazan-Dusun.

Highlights

- Participate in the Pesta Kaamatan (Harvest Festival), a lively event that includes traditional dances, music, and feasts.
- Gain insights into the Kadazan-Dusun's animistic beliefs and spiritual practices.
- Explore the beautiful countryside with local guides who share their knowledge of native plants, wildlife, and the environment.

Budget Tip

Kadazan-Dusun homestays are often available as part of larger cultural tours, which can offer additional activities like guided treks, visits to cultural centers, and cooking classes for a reasonable price.

4. Bajau Homestays (Semporna, Sabah, Malaysia)

Overview

The Bajau people, often known as the "sea gypsies," are renowned for their maritime culture, with many Bajau communities living in stilt houses or even on boats in the waters surrounding Borneo. Staying with a Bajau family provides a fascinating opportunity to experience life on the water, learn about traditional fishing methods, and enjoy fresh seafood straight from the ocean.

- **Location**: Most Bajau homestays are in Semporna, an area known for its proximity to some of the best diving spots in the world, such as Sipadan and Mabul islands.
- **Amenities**:
  - Stilt houses over the water or homes near the coastline.
  - Seafood-based meals with fish, prawns, and crabs being local favorites.
  - Activities include boat rides, snorkeling, and fishing trips.

Highlights

- Witness the Bajau people's impressive "free-diving" skills, used to harvest sea cucumbers and other marine life.
- Experience a day in the life of a Bajau fisherman, including learning how to build and maintain traditional boats.
- Explore the underwater world of the Celebes Sea with your hosts, who may offer guidance or accompany you on snorkeling excursions.

Budget Tip

Bajau homestays are often very affordable and can be combined with a dive package for great value. Make sure to book in advance during peak seasons, as accommodations can fill up quickly.

5. Rungus Homestays (Bongkud, Sabah, Malaysia)

Overview

The Rungus are known for their unique culture, which includes large communal longhouses, intricate beadwork, and elaborate traditional music and dance. Homestays with Rungus families provide travelers with an insight into the tribe's way of life and opportunities to learn about their beautiful hand-woven textiles, intricate bead designs, and agricultural practices.

- **Location**: Rungus villages are located in the northern part of Sabah, near the Kudat Peninsula.
- **Amenities**:
  - Comfortable rooms in traditional longhouses or private family homes.
  - Fresh, organic meals made from produce grown by the family, including "tinonggoh" (stewed meat and vegetables).
  - Participate in local handicraft workshops or learn to play traditional Rungus music.

Highlights

- Explore Rungus' rich history and their close ties to the land through agricultural activities and village life.
- Visit the Rungus Cultural Centre, a fascinating museum dedicated to preserving their heritage.
- Enjoy the stunning natural surroundings of the Kudat Peninsula, perfect for hiking or visiting remote beaches.

Budget Tip

Rungus homestays are often part of community tourism programs that help support the local population, so your stay directly contributes to their cultural preservation.

Final Tips for Homestays in Borneo

1. **Respect Local Customs**: Always ask before taking photos, especially of cultural ceremonies or individuals.
2. **Bring Small Gifts**: A token of appreciation is always well-received, such as food, small souvenirs, or donations to the community.
3. **Be Ready for Basic Amenities**: While homestays are incredibly enriching, be prepared for basic facilities and communal living.
4. **Communicate in Advance**: Confirm your stay ahead of time to ensure the host knows when to expect you.

By choosing to stay in a homestay, you not only gain the chance to learn from Borneo's indigenous peoples, but you also contribute to the sustainable development of these communities. It's an unforgettable way to experience the true essence of Borneo.

Chapter 5

Food and Dining: Savoring the Flavors of Borneo

Borneo's culinary scene is as vibrant and diverse as its landscapes. From aromatic spices to fresh jungle produce, every dish tells a story of tradition and heritage. Whether you're savoring a meal in a bustling city, sampling street food at a night market, or enjoying a home-cooked dish in a remote village, the flavors of Borneo promise to leave an unforgettable impression.

Traditional Dishes and Street Food Highlights

1. Nasi Lemak

A beloved Malaysian dish, Nasi Lemak is a fragrant coconut rice meal accompanied by spicy sambal, boiled eggs, fried anchovies, peanuts, and cucumber.

- **Where to Try**: Hawker stalls and eateries in Kuching and Kota Kinabalu.
- **Pro Tip**: Look for variations with fried chicken, rendang (slow-cooked beef), or fish curry for an added twist.

2. Satay

Grilled meat skewers marinated in a mix of spices and served with a rich peanut sauce.

- **Where to Try**: Night markets in cities like Kota Kinabalu and Miri.

- **Pro Tip**: Pair with ketupat (compressed rice cakes) for a full satay experience.

3. Pisang Goreng

Deep-fried bananas, a popular street snack that's crispy on the outside and soft within.

- **Where to Try**: Street vendors across Borneo.
- **Pro Tip**: Enjoy them hot with a drizzle of condensed milk or a sprinkle of cinnamon for extra indulgence.

Regional Specialties

1. Sarawak Laksa (Sarawak)

A rich, spicy noodle soup considered a culinary icon of Sarawak. It's made with rice vermicelli, shredded chicken, prawns, and a tangy tamarind-based broth.

- **Where to Try**:
  - **Chong Choon Café** in Kuching is renowned for its authentic Sarawak Laksa.
  - Local markets and food stalls in Sarawak.
- **Pro Tip**: For a true Sarawak Laksa experience, pair your bowl with a cup of Teh C Peng Special, a layered iced tea drink.

2. Hinava (Sabah)

A Kadazan-Dusun specialty, Hinava is a type of raw fish salad made with fresh fish (usually mackerel), lime juice, ginger, shallots, chili, and grated bambangan (a local sour fruit).

- **Where to Try**:
  - Homestays in Sabah, where locals prepare it fresh.

- Restaurants that specialize in Kadazan-Dusun cuisine, such as *D'Place Kinabalu*.
- **Pro Tip**: This dish is best enjoyed as an appetizer and pairs excellently with plain rice or traditional rice wine (tapai).

3. Ayam Pansuh (Sarawak)

A dish where chicken is marinated with herbs, stuffed into bamboo tubes, and cooked over an open flame, infusing it with a smoky aroma and a tender texture.

- **Where to Try**:
  - Indigenous villages during traditional festivals.
  - Restaurants offering Dayak cuisine in Kuching.
- **Pro Tip**: Ask for a serving of jungle ferns (midin) as a side dish—it complements Ayam Pansuh perfectly.

Other Must-Try Dishes

1. Ambuyat (Brunei and Sabah)

A starchy dish made from sago palm starch, served with a variety of dips and side dishes. It has a glue-like consistency and is eaten by twirling it around chopsticks.

- **Where to Try**:
  - Local restaurants in Brunei.
  - Traditional feasts in Sabah.
- **Pro Tip**: Pair it with sour and spicy sauces like cencaluk (fermented shrimp sauce) for a burst of flavor.

2. Manok Pansoh (Sarawak)

A variation of bamboo-cooked chicken that uses a mix of wild ginger, garlic, and chili for a fragrant and flavorful meal.

- **Where to Try**:
  - Longhouse stays in rural Sarawak.
  - Special Dayak cultural events.
- **Pro Tip**: Complement this dish with tuak (local rice wine) for a traditional experience.

3. Tuaran Mee (Sabah)

A stir-fried noodle dish unique to the town of Tuaran, featuring egg noodles, pork, vegetables, and eggs.

- **Where to Try**:
  - Hawker centers in Tuaran and Kota Kinabalu.
  - Restaurants such as *Mee Tuaran Restaurant*.
- **Pro Tip**: Look for variations with seafood for an elevated taste experience.

Tips for Foodies Exploring Borneo

1. **Street Food Etiquette**: While street food is delicious and affordable, choose vendors with high turnover for the freshest dishes.
2. **Spice Levels**: Many Bornean dishes are spicy. If you're sensitive to heat, ask for "kurang pedas" (less spicy) when ordering.
3. **Vegetarian Options**: While meat and seafood dominate Bornean cuisine, vegetarian dishes like stir-fried vegetables with garlic, tofu, and jungle ferns are widely available.
4. **Local Fruits**: Don't miss tropical delights like rambutan, durian, langsat, and mangosteen, often sold at roadside stalls.

5. **Water Safety**: Stick to bottled water and avoid drinks with ice unless you're confident about the water quality.

Whether you're dining in bustling cities, remote villages, or serene rainforest lodges, the culinary journey in Borneo is one of discovery and delight. From fiery sambals to fragrant noodles soups, every bite is a celebration of the island's rich cultural tapestry.

Fine Dining: Fusion Cuisine and Modern Borneo Restaurants

Borneo's fine dining scene seamlessly combines traditional flavors with contemporary culinary trends. Restaurants across the island creatively showcase the richness of local ingredients, crafting unforgettable dining experiences for those seeking a taste of modern Borneo.

Fusion Cuisine and Modern Borneo Restaurants

1. The Waterfront Café & Restaurant (Kuching, Sarawak)

A sophisticated venue overlooking the Sarawak River, this restaurant is known for its modern take on traditional dishes. Their reinterpretations of Sarawak Laksa and Ayam Pansuh are a must-try.

- **Signature Dishes**: Grilled river prawns with sambal butter, bamboo-smoked chicken.
- **Ambiance**: Chic and tranquil with open-air seating by the river.
- **Pro Tip**: Reserve a table for sunset views over the river, and pair your meal with a Sarawak pepper-infused cocktail.

2. Nook (Aloft Kota Kinabalu, Sabah)

Blending local Sabah flavors with international flair, Nook offers a dining experience that's both upscale and rooted in Bornean traditions.

- **Signature Dishes**: Hinava ceviche, sous-vide lamb with tuhau (wild ginger).
- **Ambiance**: Sleek, modern interiors with panoramic city views.
- **Pro Tip**: Visit during special themed nights featuring live music and chef's specials inspired by seasonal ingredients.

3. Kaizen Sushi (Bandar Seri Begawan, Brunei)

For seafood lovers, this restaurant fuses Japanese cuisine with Bornean seafood. Fresh sushi and sashimi are complemented by unique items like tempura soft-shell crab with a sambal twist.

- **Signature Dishes**: Borneo lobster sushi roll, unagi sambal maki.
- **Ambiance**: Minimalist and elegant, with a focus on the artistry of the dishes.
- **Pro Tip**: Order their tasting menu for a curated exploration of their best dishes.

4. Makan Street by Hilton (Kota Kinabalu, Sabah)

A luxurious yet approachable restaurant that offers a modern twist on street food classics, taking you on a culinary journey through Sabah.

- **Signature Dishes**: Charcoal-grilled satay skewers, laksa ravioli.
- **Ambiance**: Casual fine dining with vibrant décor inspired by local markets.
- **Pro Tip**: Indulge in their dessert selection, featuring pandan-infused crème brûlée and durian parfait.

Insider's Guide to the Best Food Markets

For an authentic taste of Borneo, food markets offer a sensory overload of vibrant sights, tantalizing aromas, and bold flavors. Here's where you can find the best markets to immerse yourself in Borneo's culinary culture:

1. Gaya Street Sunday Market (Kota Kinabalu, Sabah)

A sprawling market that comes alive every Sunday morning, offering everything from fresh produce to sizzling street food.

- **Must-Try Dishes**:
  - Grilled fish wrapped in banana leaves.
  - Coconut pudding served in a coconut shell.
- **Insider Tip**: Arrive early to beat the crowds and enjoy freshly cooked breakfast options like apam balik (crispy peanut pancakes).

2. Top Spot Food Court (Kuching, Sarawak)

This iconic food market is famous for its fresh seafood and communal dining atmosphere. Dozens of stalls compete to serve up the best of Borneo's marine bounty.

- **Must-Try Dishes**:
  - Butter prawns with curry leaves.
  - Midin (jungle fern) stir-fried with belacan (shrimp paste).
- **Insider Tip**: Look for stalls with long lines—they're popular for a reason. Don't miss the salted egg crab!

3. Tamu Kianggeh Market (Bandar Seri Begawan, Brunei)

A bustling local market offering a mix of fresh ingredients and ready-to-eat meals. It's a great place to discover Brunei's culinary staples.

- **Must-Try Dishes**:
  - Nasi katok (rice with fried chicken and sambal).
  - Ambuyat with an assortment of dips.
- **Insider Tip**: Engage with the vendors to learn about the ingredients and recipes—they're usually happy to share!

4. Siniawan Night Market (Sarawak)

A quaint weekend market held in a historic shophouse village, offering a charming mix of local dishes and international flavors.

- **Must-Try Dishes**:
  - Handmade dumplings.
  - Smoked pork belly.
- **Insider Tip**: This market is family-friendly and often features live music for a delightful evening experience.

5. Pasar Filipina (Filipino Market, Kota Kinabalu, Sabah)

A vibrant market by the waterfront, famous for its fresh seafood and lively atmosphere.

- **Must-Try Dishes**:
  - Grilled squid.
  - Fresh coconut juice.
- **Insider Tip**: Haggle with seafood vendors for the best price, and they'll grill your purchase right on the spot.

Tips for Navigating Food Markets in Borneo

1. **Bring Cash**: Many stalls don't accept credit cards, so carry small denominations of local currency.
2. **Stay Hydrated**: Markets can get hot and humid—fresh coconut water is a refreshing option.

3. **Sample Before You Buy**: Vendors often offer small samples, especially for fruits and snacks.
4. **Mind Hygiene**: Choose stalls with clean cooking setups and high customer turnover for the freshest and safest food.

From lavish fine dining experiences to bustling food markets, Borneo offers culinary adventures for every taste and budget. Whether you're indulging in a five-star fusion meal or savoring a smoky grilled satay at a market, the flavors of Borneo are sure to captivate your palate and enrich your journey.

Dear Reader,

Thank you for choosing *Borneo Travel Guide 2025*. It's been an honor to guide you through the breathtaking landscapes, rich culture, and unforgettable experiences of this incredible island. I hope this book has sparked your curiosity, answered your questions, and left you eager to explore everything Borneo has to offer.

Your thoughts and feelings about this book mean so much to me.

- Did you find what you were looking for?
- Was there a part that truly stood out or made you dream about your journey?
- Is there something you'd love to see added or explored further?

I'd love to hear from you! Your insights will help me grow and ensure future editions are even more helpful and inspiring for readers like you.

If you found this guide helpful, I'd be so grateful if you'd share it with your friends, family, or anyone dreaming of visiting Borneo. A kind recommendation can inspire someone else to experience this magical destination. 🌿

Thank you for allowing me to be part of your travel journey. Wishing you endless wonder and adventure ahead!

Warmly,
Julian D. Cross

Chapter 6

Must-Visit Landmarks in Borneo

Mount Kinabalu: The Crown Jewel of Sabah

Rising to a staggering 4,095 meters, **Mount Kinabalu** is not just the tallest mountain in Borneo but also one of the most iconic landmarks in Southeast Asia. Its majestic silhouette dominates the landscape of Sabah, making it a beacon for adventurers and nature enthusiasts from around the globe. Recognized as a UNESCO World Heritage Site, Mount Kinabalu is a biodiversity hotspot and a spiritual centerpiece for the indigenous Kadazan-Dusun people.

Why Visit Mount Kinabalu?

1. Awe-Inspiring Scenery

Mount Kinabalu offers breathtaking views that evolve as you ascend. From lush tropical forests at the base to alpine meadows and rocky granite peaks at the summit, every step reveals nature's artistry. The sunrise view from the peak is a life-changing experience, as the first rays of light illuminate the surrounding clouds and valleys.

2. A Biodiversity Treasure Trove

The mountain and its surrounding park are home to an astonishing array of flora and fauna, many of which are endemic to the region. Highlights include:

- **Rafflesia Arnoldii**: The world's largest flower, a rare and fascinating plant.
- **Nepenthes Rajah**: A giant pitcher plant found only on Mount Kinabalu.

- **Birdlife**: Over 300 bird species, including the mountain black-eye and Bornean treepie.

3. Spiritual Significance

For the indigenous Kadazan-Dusun people, Mount Kinabalu is a sacred site believed to be the resting place of their ancestors' spirits. This reverence adds an element of mystique and cultural depth to the climb.

Climbing Mount Kinabalu

The Climb

Mount Kinabalu offers a thrilling yet manageable climb that attracts both seasoned hikers and beginners. The **Summit Trail**, starting at Timpohon Gate, is the most popular route to the peak.

Key Information for Climbers

- **Duration**: The trek typically takes two days.
- **Base Camp**: Climbers stay overnight at **Panalaban Base Camp**, located 3,272 meters above sea level.
- **Difficulty**: Moderate, but climbers must be prepared for steep inclines and thinner air as they ascend.

Highlights Along the Trail

- **Carson's Falls**: A picturesque waterfall near the beginning of the trail.
- **Layang-Layang Point**: A great spot for a rest with panoramic views.
- **Low's Peak**: The summit, named after British colonial administrator Hugh Low, offers unmatched sunrise views.

What You Need to Know Before You Go

Permits and Booking

Climbing Mount Kinabalu requires a permit, guide, and accommodations at the base camp, all of which are managed by the **Sabah Parks Authority**. These must be booked in advance due to limited availability.

Fitness Requirements

While the climb is non-technical, it demands a good level of physical fitness. Acclimatization to high altitudes is also recommended to avoid altitude sickness.

Essential Gear

- Warm clothing for the summit climb.
- Sturdy trekking shoes.
- Headlamp (for the pre-dawn ascent).
- Snacks and a reusable water bottle.

Beyond the Summit: Exploring Kinabalu Park

Kinabalu Park, the gateway to Mount Kinabalu, is a natural wonder in its own right. Spanning over 750 square kilometers, it features:

- **Nature Trails**: Well-marked paths for casual hikers, such as the **Bukit Tupai Trail** and the **Kiau View Trail**.
- **Botanical Gardens**: A curated collection of the park's rich plant life, including orchids and ferns.
- **Poring Hot Springs**: Perfect for post-climb relaxation, these natural hot springs soothe tired muscles.

Pro Tips for a Memorable Visit

1. **Book Early**: Climbing slots are limited and fill up months in advance, especially during peak seasons (March to May).
2. **Time Your Visit**: The best time to climb is during the dry season (March to September) for clearer skies.
3. **Guides are Essential**: All climbers must be accompanied by a licensed guide, who also shares insights about the mountain's ecology and culture.
4. **Respect the Mountain**: Observe rules and respect the spiritual significance of the site. Leave no trace behind.

Mount Kinabalu is more than just a mountain; it's a journey into Borneo's heart and soul. From its unparalleled biodiversity to its cultural and spiritual significance, a visit to this natural wonder promises an adventure you'll never forget. Whether you seek personal triumph in reaching the summit or simply want to bask in its natural beauty, Mount Kinabalu awaits as the crown jewel of Sabah.

Kinabatangan River: Sabah's Wildlife Paradise

Nestled in the heart of Sabah, the **Kinabatangan River** stretches over 560 kilometers, making it Malaysia's second-longest river. Renowned for its astonishing biodiversity and unique ecosystems, the Kinabatangan River has become a haven for wildlife enthusiasts, offering unparalleled opportunities to witness Borneo's extraordinary flora and fauna.

Why Visit the Kinabatangan River?

1. A Biodiversity Hotspot

The Kinabatangan River basin is one of the richest ecosystems in the world. This lowland rainforest is home to some of Borneo's most iconic wildlife, including:

- **Bornean Pygmy Elephants**: The world's smallest elephant species, often seen grazing along the riverbanks.
- **Proboscis Monkeys**: Endemic to Borneo, these quirky primates with large noses are often spotted in trees near the water.
- **Orangutans**: Swinging through the canopy, these gentle great apes are a true highlight.
- **Exotic Birds**: Hornbills, kingfishers, and eagles are just some of the 200+ bird species that call this area home.

2. Stunning Landscapes

The Kinabatangan River offers a mix of habitats, including mangroves, swamp forests, and oxbow lakes. These create an ever-changing backdrop for wildlife encounters.

3. Unique Ecosystems

This region is one of the few places in the world where limestone caves, freshwater swamps, and rainforest ecosystems converge, making it a living laboratory of natural wonders.

Activities Along the Kinabatangan River

1. River Safaris

The main draw of the Kinabatangan is its river cruises, which take you deep into the heart of this ecological gem.

- **Dawn Cruises**: The best time to see wildlife as the river comes alive with activity.
- **Dusk Cruises**: Perfect for spotting nocturnal animals emerging from their hiding places.
- **Night Cruises**: A magical experience, with glowing fireflies lighting up the mangroves.

2. Jungle Trekking

Explore the dense rainforest on foot, guided by experienced locals who reveal the hidden treasures of the jungle, from medicinal plants to tiny, elusive creatures.

3. Birdwatching

With over 200 species of birds, including all eight species of Borneo's hornbills, the Kinabatangan River is a paradise for ornithologists and birding enthusiasts.

4. Visiting Oxbow Lakes

These crescent-shaped lakes, formed from meanders in the river, are serene spots for birdwatching and picnics.

How to Experience Kinabatangan River

Where to Stay

- **Eco-Lodges**: Sustainable accommodations such as **Sukau Rainforest Lodge** and **Kinabatangan Riverside Lodge** offer comfortable stays with a minimal environmental footprint.
- **Homestays**: For a more authentic experience, stay with local families in villages like Sukau and Bilit.

Best Time to Visit

The dry season from **March to October** is ideal, as the lower water levels make wildlife sightings along the riverbanks more frequent.

What to Pack for Your Kinabatangan Adventure

- **Binoculars**: Essential for spotting wildlife from a distance.
- **Lightweight Clothing**: Preferably long-sleeved for protection from insects.
- **Waterproof Gear**: Rain is frequent, even during the dry season.
- **Insect Repellent**: A must for keeping mosquitoes at bay.

Pro Tips for a Memorable Visit

1. **Book a Guided Tour**: Experienced guides enhance your chances of spotting elusive wildlife and share fascinating insights about the ecosystem.
2. **Timing is Key**: Opt for dawn or dusk cruises for optimal wildlife activity.
3. **Stay Quiet**: Minimize noise during safaris to avoid scaring away animals.
4. **Respect Nature**: Do not feed or disturb wildlife, and always follow local guidelines to protect this fragile ecosystem.

Nearby Attractions

While visiting the Kinabatangan River, consider exploring other nearby attractions:

- **Gomantong Caves**: Famous for their edible bird's nests and colonies of bats.
- **Danum Valley**: A pristine rainforest with more opportunities for wildlife spotting and trekking.

The Kinabatangan River offers a unique blend of adventure, relaxation, and discovery. Whether you're gliding along its calm waters or trekking through its dense jungles, the experience promises to immerse you in the incredible natural beauty and wildlife of Borneo. For nature lovers and adventurers alike, the Kinabatangan River is a journey into one of Earth's last great wild frontiers.

73

Mulu Caves: A Subterranean Marvel in Sarawak

Hidden deep within the lush rainforests of Sarawak, the **Mulu Caves** are one of Borneo's most extraordinary natural wonders. Located within the **Gunung Mulu National Park**, a UNESCO World Heritage Site, these caves are famed for their immense size, intricate formations, and unique ecosystems. The park is a must-visit for nature lovers, adventure seekers, and those intrigued by the mysteries of the underground world.

Why Visit Mulu Caves?

1. Home to Record-Breaking Caves

The Mulu Caves are home to some of the most impressive cave systems in the world, including:

- **Sarawak Chamber**: The world's largest cave chamber, capable of fitting over 40 Boeing 747 airplanes.
- **Deer Cave**: One of the largest cave passages in the world, renowned for its colossal size and the nightly exodus of millions of bats.
- **Clearwater Cave**: A stunning underground river system that is part of one of the longest caves in the world.

2. The Nightly Bat Exodus

Deer Cave is famous for the incredible spectacle of millions of bats emerging at dusk in search of food. The swirling, synchronized movements of the bat exodus against the evening sky are mesmerizing and a photographer's dream.

3. Unique Ecosystems

Each cave features its own distinct environment, from glowworm-lit chambers to underground rivers teeming with life. Above ground, Gunung Mulu National Park boasts rich biodiversity, with over 3,500 plant species, including the rare pitcher plant and giant dipterocarp trees.

Activities in and Around Mulu Caves

1. Cave Exploration

There are caves for every type of visitor:

- **Show Caves**: Accessible via guided tours, Deer Cave and Lang Cave showcase awe-inspiring rock formations and wildlife.
- **Adventure Caving**: For thrill-seekers, explore less-traveled caves like Racer Cave, where you'll rappel, crawl, and climb.
- **Clearwater Cave**: Enjoy a boat ride to this cave and marvel at its underground river system.

2. Canopy Walks

The **Mulu Canopy Walk** is one of the world's longest tree-based walkways, offering stunning views of the rainforest and a chance to spot birds and monkeys in the treetops.

3. Jungle Trekking

The park offers numerous trails, ranging from short hikes to multi-day treks like the challenging climb to **The Pinnacles**, razor-sharp limestone formations atop Mount Api.

What You Need to Know

Getting to Mulu

The easiest way to reach Gunung Mulu National Park is by air. Direct flights are available from Miri, Kuching, and Kota Kinabalu to **Mulu Airport**. The park is remote, with no roads connecting it to major towns, making flying the most convenient option.

Where to Stay

- **Mulu Marriott Resort & Spa**: Offers luxury accommodations near the park.
- **National Park Lodges**: Comfortable and affordable, located within the park itself.
- **Local Homestays**: For a more immersive experience, stay with locals in nearby villages.

When to Visit

The best time to visit is during the dry season, from **March to September**, when trails are less muddy, and cave tours are less likely to be disrupted by rain.

What to Bring

- **Sturdy Footwear**: Essential for slippery cave floors and rugged jungle trails.
- **Flashlight or Headlamp**: While show caves are well-lit, adventure caves require personal lighting.
- **Bug Spray**: To keep mosquitoes and other insects at bay.
- **Rain Gear**: Sudden downpours are common in the rainforest.

Pro Tips for Visiting Mulu Caves

1. **Book Tours in Advance**: Slots for cave tours and canopy walks are limited, so early booking is recommended.
2. **Prepare for Adventure**: Adventure caving tours can be physically demanding, so a good level of fitness is essential.
3. **Respect the Environment**: Avoid touching cave formations, as they take thousands of years to form, and always follow your guide's instructions.
4. **Plan for the Bat Exodus**: Arrive early at the Deer Cave observation deck to secure a good viewing spot.

Nearby Attractions

While in the area, consider exploring these additional highlights:

- **The Pinnacles**: A challenging hike with stunning limestone spires at the summit.
- **Wind Cave**: Known for its cool breezes and striking stalactites and stalagmites.
- **Melinau Gorge**: A picturesque river gorge near Clearwater Cave.

The Mulu Caves are not just a destination but a journey into the heart of Borneo's geological and ecological marvels. Whether you're a casual traveler seeking awe-inspiring sights or a hardcore adventurer eager to delve into hidden chambers, the Mulu Caves offer an unforgettable experience. From the grandeur of the Sarawak Chamber to the natural drama of the bat exodus, this is a place where nature's power and beauty converge in spectacular fashion.

Sepilok Orangutan Rehabilitation Centre: A Sanctuary for Borneo's Icons

Located in the verdant heart of **Sabah**, the **Sepilok Orangutan Rehabilitation Centre** is one of Borneo's most celebrated conservation efforts. Established in 1964, it serves as a haven for orphaned, injured, and displaced orangutans, offering them a chance to recover and eventually return to the wild. For travelers seeking an up-close encounter with these intelligent primates in a semi-natural setting, Sepilok provides an unforgettable and educational experience.

Why Visit Sepilok Orangutan Rehabilitation Centre?

1. Conservation in Action

Sepilok's primary mission is to rehabilitate orangutans affected by deforestation, illegal pet trade, and human-wildlife conflict. Visitors can witness these efforts firsthand, observing young orangutans in their journey to independence.

2. Semi-Wild Environment

Unlike zoos, the orangutans roam freely within a 4,300-hectare protected rainforest reserve. This provides a unique opportunity to see them exhibiting natural behaviors in their native habitat.

3. Connection to Sabah's Wildlife

Sepilok is part of the **Kabili-Sepilok Forest Reserve**, which supports a wide range of wildlife, including macaques, sun bears, and over 250 bird species.

Highlights of Your Visit

1. Feeding Sessions

Twice daily, at **10:00 AM** and **3:00 PM**, visitors can observe orangutans as they come to the feeding platforms for a meal of fruits and vegetables. While the food attracts the primates, it's kept intentionally basic to encourage foraging in the forest.

- **Pro Tip**: Arrive at least 30 minutes early to secure a prime viewing spot, especially during peak tourist seasons.

2. Outdoor Nursery

The nursery area provides a heartwarming view of young orangutans learning crucial survival skills, such as climbing and swinging, under the watchful eyes of their caregivers.

3. Rainforest Discovery Centre (RDC)

Located nearby, the RDC complements your visit with canopy walkways, botanical gardens, and educational exhibits on Borneo's unique flora and fauna.

How to Experience Sepilok Orangutan Rehabilitation Centre

Admission and Access

- **Opening Hours**: 9:00 AM to 12:00 PM and 2:00 PM to 4:00 PM daily.
- **Entrance Fees**:
    - Adults: RM 30
    - Children: RM 15
    - Camera Fees: RM 10 (for photography enthusiasts).
- **Location**: About 25 kilometers from Sandakan, Sepilok is easily accessible by road or taxi.

Best Time to Visit

The center is open year-round, but the dry season from **March to October** offers more comfortable conditions for exploration.

Where to Stay

- **Sepilok Nature Resort**: A charming lodge nestled amidst the rainforest, just steps away from the center.
- **Sandakan Accommodations**: For budget options, Sandakan offers various hotels and guesthouses with easy access to Sepilok.

What to Bring

- **Comfortable Walking Shoes**: Trails to the feeding platforms and nursery are well-maintained but may be slippery after rain.
- **Insect Repellent**: To ward off mosquitoes in the rainforest.
- **Binoculars**: For birdwatching and spotting wildlife in the reserve.
- **Water Bottle**: Stay hydrated while exploring.

Pro Tips for Visiting Sepilok

1. **Respect Wildlife**: Maintain a safe distance and avoid making loud noises or sudden movements.
2. **Avoid Feeding the Animals**: Feeding orangutans or other wildlife can disrupt their rehabilitation process.
3. **Plan for Rain**: Sudden tropical showers are common, so pack a raincoat or poncho.

Nearby Attractions

Combine your visit to Sepilok with other exciting destinations in the region:

- **Bornean Sun Bear Conservation Centre**: Located adjacent to Sepilok, this center focuses on the protection of the world's smallest bear species.
- **Labuk Bay Proboscis Monkey Sanctuary**: Witness the peculiar proboscis monkeys in their natural mangrove habitat.
- **Gomantong Caves**: Explore these fascinating caves known for their edible bird's nests.

An Unforgettable Wildlife Experience

The Sepilok Orangutan Rehabilitation Centre offers more than just a chance to see orangutans—it provides an intimate look into the challenges of conservation in Borneo. Whether you're captivated by the orangutans' playful antics or moved by the dedication of the staff, your visit to Sepilok will undoubtedly leave a lasting impression and deepen your appreciation for Borneo's unique wildlife and ecosystems.

Brunei's Omar Ali Saifuddien Mosque: A Masterpiece of Islamic Architecture

Nestled in the heart of **Bandar Seri Begawan**, the capital of Brunei, the **Omar Ali Saifuddien Mosque** stands as a magnificent symbol of the nation's Islamic heritage, cultural pride, and wealth. Named after Sultan Omar Ali Saifuddien III, the 28th Sultan of Brunei, this mosque is a spiritual and architectural landmark that seamlessly blends traditional Islamic design with modern elegance.

Why Visit the Omar Ali Saifuddien Mosque?

1. Architectural Grandeur

The mosque's opulence is apparent in its design, which features materials sourced from around the globe. The stunning golden dome, Italian marble, English stained glass, Saudi Arabian carpets, and crystal chandeliers come together to create a visual feast.

2. Lagoon and Ceremonial Barge

The mosque is surrounded by a serene, man-made lagoon, enhancing its picturesque appeal. A replica of a **16th-century ceremonial barge** floats gracefully on the lagoon, adding to the mosque's grandeur.

3. Cultural and Religious Significance

More than just a visual marvel, the mosque represents Brunei's dedication to preserving Islamic values and cultural heritage.

Highlights of Your Visit

1. Stunning Interiors

Step inside to admire intricate calligraphy, finely carved marble walls, and soaring arches. The prayer hall, reserved for male worshippers, is adorned with luxurious carpets and ornate details, showcasing Brunei's craftsmanship.

2. The Golden Dome

Visible from various parts of the city, the iconic golden dome gleams under the tropical sun and stands as a testament to Brunei's prosperity.

3. The Lagoon and Barge

Take a leisurely stroll around the lagoon to appreciate the mosque's reflection in the water. The ceremonial barge, once used for Quranic recitations, is a popular photography spot.

4. Evening Views

At dusk, the mosque is illuminated, casting its shimmering reflection on the lagoon. This creates a magical atmosphere and a prime opportunity for stunning photographs.

Plan Your Visit

Opening Hours

- Visitors are welcome **outside prayer times**.
- **Non-Muslims** are not permitted during Friday prayers or religious ceremonies.

Entry Fees

- **Free of charge**, though donations for upkeep are appreciated.

Dress Code

- Modest clothing is mandatory. Long sleeves and trousers or skirts covering the knees are recommended. Robes are provided for visitors if needed.

How to Get There

- **By Car**: Located in the city center, the mosque is easily accessible via private car or taxi.
- **By Foot**: For visitors staying in **Bandar Seri Begawan**, the mosque is within walking distance of major hotels and landmarks.
- **Public Transport**: Buses and shuttles connect to the city center from the airport and other districts.

What to Bring

- **Camera**: Photography is allowed in the outdoor areas but is restricted inside the mosque.
- **Comfortable Shoes**: Shoes must be removed before entering, so ensure yours are easy to slip off.
- **Sunscreen or Umbrella**: The tropical sun can be intense during the day.

Nearby Attractions

After visiting the Omar Ali Saifuddien Mosque, consider exploring these nearby sites:

- **Royal Regalia Museum**: Dive into Brunei's royal history and admire the opulent artifacts.
- **Kampong Ayer**: Known as the "Venice of the East," this water village offers a glimpse into traditional Bruneian life.
- **Taman Mahkota Jubli Emas**: A riverside park perfect for a leisurely walk and panoramic views of the mosque.

Pro Tips for an Enriching Visit

1. **Visit at Sunset**: The mosque's golden dome takes on a mesmerizing glow, and the lagoon's reflections are at their most enchanting.
2. **Respect Local Customs**: Be mindful of Brunei's conservative Islamic culture and adhere to etiquette during your visit.
3. **Combine with a Guided Tour**: Local guides provide in-depth knowledge about the mosque's history, architecture, and cultural significance.

An Icon of Brunei's Elegance

The Omar Ali Saifuddien Mosque is more than just a religious site; it is a breathtaking example of Islamic artistry and a reflection of Brunei's harmonious blend of tradition and modernity. Whether you're an architecture enthusiast, a cultural explorer, or simply seeking moments of serenity, a visit to this majestic mosque will undoubtedly leave you inspired and in awe of its timeless beauty.

Danum Valley Conservation Area: A Pristine Rainforest Paradise

The **Danum Valley Conservation Area**, nestled deep in the heart of Sabah, Malaysia, is a 438-square-kilometer expanse of undisturbed lowland rainforest. Renowned for its extraordinary biodiversity and untouched landscapes, it is a sanctuary for rare and endangered species and a dream destination for nature lovers, researchers, and eco-adventurers.

Why Visit the Danum Valley Conservation Area?

1. Biodiversity Hotspot

Home to over 500 species of birds, 124 species of mammals, 200 species of plants per hectare, and countless insects, Danum Valley is a naturalist's utopia. Rare sightings of **clouded leopards**, **Bornean orangutans**, and the elusive **Bornean pygmy elephants** make every trek an adventure.

2. Pristine Ecosystem

As one of the last remaining untouched rainforests in Southeast Asia, Danum Valley offers an unparalleled glimpse into what tropical rainforests were like millions of years ago.

3. Unique Activities

Visitors can enjoy canopy walks, night safaris, and river excursions, all while soaking in the beauty of a living, breathing rainforest.

Highlights of Your Visit

1. Canopy Walks

- Walk through towering treetops on **suspension bridges** offering breathtaking views of the jungle canopy.
- Spot treetop species like **hornbills**, **gibbons**, and vibrant butterflies.

2. Night Safaris

- Embark on guided night tours to encounter nocturnal animals, such as **civet cats**, **leopard cats**, and glowing fungi.
- The sounds of the rainforest at night are a symphony of nature that's both thrilling and enchanting.

3. Ancient Burial Sites

- Visit sites with **Kadazandusun burial coffins**, placed high in limestone caves, offering a glimpse into the indigenous communities' spiritual traditions.

4. Rare Wildlife Sightings

- Witness the natural behaviors of iconic species like **orangutans** and **proboscis monkeys**.
- Keep an eye out for the elusive **clouded leopard**, one of the rainforest's most mysterious predators.

Plan Your Visit

Best Time to Visit

- The **dry season** (March to October) is ideal for trekking and wildlife spotting, though the rainforest's lush greenery makes it a year-round destination.

Entry Requirements

- Access to Danum Valley is highly regulated to protect the ecosystem. Book your stay at authorized accommodations to arrange entry.

Travel Packages

- Many packages include guided treks, night safaris, and transportation from nearby towns like Lahad Datu.

Where to Stay

1. Danum Valley Field Centre

- This research hub offers simple accommodations for eco-conscious travelers and researchers.
- Gain insight into ongoing conservation efforts and immerse yourself in the heart of the rainforest.

2. Borneo Rainforest Lodge

- A luxurious option featuring private chalets, outdoor tubs, and guided tours. Ideal for travelers seeking comfort amidst the wild.

How to Get There

- **By Air**: Fly to **Lahad Datu Airport**, the closest access point.
- **By Road**: A 2-hour 4WD journey from Lahad Datu brings you to Danum Valley.
- **By Guided Tours**: Opt for tour packages from **Kota Kinabalu** or **Sandakan**, which include transportation and activities

---

What to Bring

- **Hiking Boots**: Essential for navigating uneven trails.
- **Insect Repellent**: The dense rainforest is teeming with insects, including mosquitoes.
- **Rain Gear**: Weather can change rapidly in the jungle.
- **Binoculars**: Perfect for spotting birds and distant wildlife.

Pro Tips for an Unforgettable Experience

1. **Stay Longer for Wildlife**
   - A minimum of 2–3 days increases your chances of spotting rare animals.
2. **Hire a Guide**
   - Local guides are invaluable for spotting elusive wildlife and sharing their deep knowledge of the ecosystem.

3. **Respect the Environment**
   - ○ Stay on designated trails and avoid disturbing animals to help preserve this precious habitat.

Nearby Attractions

- **Tabin Wildlife Reserve**: Known for its mud volcanoes and rich biodiversity.
- **Maliau Basin**: Dubbed the "Lost World of Sabah," this remote area is another haven for adventurers.

The Ultimate Rainforest Adventure

The Danum Valley Conservation Area is a testament to the beauty and importance of untouched ecosystems. Whether you're a seasoned adventurer, a wildlife enthusiast, or a casual traveler seeking a connection with nature, this rainforest paradise offers an experience that will leave you humbled, inspired, and profoundly grateful for the wonders of our natural world.

Kuching Waterfront and Fort Margherita: A Journey Through History and Culture

Kuching, the capital city of **Sarawak**, Malaysia, is often referred to as the "Cat City," owing to its rich history and the many cat statues dotted throughout the city. Situated on the banks of the **Sarawak River**, the **Kuching Waterfront** is a vibrant hub, offering a blend of scenic views, cultural landmarks, and local experiences. Just across the river, perched majestically on a hill, lies the **Fort Margherita**, an important historical site that provides a fascinating glimpse into Sarawak's past during the Brooke era.

Why Visit Kuching Waterfront and Fort Margherita?

1. A Unique Blend of Nature and Culture

Kuching's waterfront is a cultural and social hotspot where nature meets history. Visitors can relax by the riverside, indulge in local cuisine, take river cruises, and explore the vibrant street markets. In contrast, Fort Margherita offers a quiet retreat with panoramic views of the river and a glimpse into the colonial past of the region.

2. Sarawak's Fascinating History

Fort Margherita stands as a testament to the legacy of the **Brooke family**, who ruled Sarawak for over a century. Built in 1879 by **Charles Brooke**, the second White Rajah, the fort was originally intended to protect the city from pirates and insurgents. Today, it houses the **Brooke Gallery**, which offers valuable insights into the region's history under the Brookes.

Highlights of Kuching Waterfront

1. Scenic River Cruises

- Hop on a **Sarawak River Cruise** for a unique perspective of the city, where you can enjoy views of the **Malay villages**, lush landscapes, and historical buildings lining the banks.
- The cruise is especially enchanting at sunset, offering breathtaking views as the sky turns golden.
- **Pro Tip**: Opt for evening cruises for a stunning view of Kuching's skyline illuminated by the setting sun.

2. Street Food and Local Delights

- Along the waterfront, you'll find an array of food stalls offering local delicacies, such as **kolo mee**, **laksa**, and **soto ayam**.
- For dessert, try **cendol** or **kuih**—traditional Malaysian sweets that perfectly complement the warm tropical climate.
- **Pro Tip**: Stop by the bustling **Kuching Waterfront Night Market** for a lively food scene, offering everything from savory snacks to sweet treats.

3. Riverside Promenade

- The **Kuching Waterfront Promenade** is a perfect place to relax, people-watch, or take a leisurely stroll. The pathway is lined with **modern sculptures**, **green spaces**, and **palm trees**, offering a peaceful escape.
- **Pro Tip**: Visit in the evening for a cooler atmosphere, as locals and tourists gather along the waterfront to enjoy the balmy night air.

4. The Square Tower and Tua Pek Kong Temple

- Nearby the waterfront, you'll also find the **Square Tower**, a historic building that once served as a fort and prison. The **Tua**

Pek Kong Temple, an ornate and colorful Chinese temple, adds to the charm of the area, showcasing the city's diverse cultural heritage.

Highlights of Fort Margherita

1. The Brooke Gallery

- Inside **Fort Margherita**, the **Brooke Gallery** provides a deep dive into the history of Sarawak's colonial era.
- Explore exhibits that showcase the **Brooke family**, their rule over Sarawak, and the fort's role in protecting the city.
- Learn about the exploits of **James Brooke**, the first White Rajah, and his successors, who transformed Sarawak into a prosperous kingdom.
- **Pro Tip**: Visit the gallery for a well-rounded historical context before embarking on a river cruise to fully appreciate the area's colonial significance.

2. Views from the Fort

- Situated on a hill overlooking the **Sarawak River**, Fort Margherita offers panoramic views of the river and Kuching city. The vantage point from the fort is one of the best in the city, perfect for capturing memorable photos.
- **Pro Tip**: Arrive early in the morning or later in the afternoon to avoid crowds and to enjoy the tranquil views.

3. Historic Architecture

- The fort is a classic example of British colonial military architecture. Its design includes **a large clock tower, bastions, and iron cannons** that reflect its original purpose as a defensive structure.

- **Pro Tip**: Take time to explore the fort's exterior to appreciate its architectural details before heading inside to the gallery.

Pro Tips for Visiting Kuching Waterfront and Fort Margherita

1. Evening Walks for a Vibrant Atmosphere

- The evening transforms the Kuching Waterfront into a vibrant social scene, with **live music performances**, **local artisans selling handmade goods**, and **street performers** entertaining the crowds.
- **Pro Tip**: Visit around **7:00 PM** when the atmosphere is at its liveliest, and enjoy a walk along the waterfront while watching the sunset.

2. Combine History with Relaxation

- After exploring Fort Margherita, take a relaxing walk along the **waterfront promenade**, stopping at **local cafés** and enjoying a refreshing drink.
- Don't forget to catch the **night market** for some local snacks and unique souvenirs.

3. Visit During the Festivals

- If you happen to visit Kuching during one of its many festivals, such as the **Gawai Dayak Festival** (a harvest celebration) or the **Rainforest World Music Festival**, the Waterfront area becomes the heart of the festivities.
- **Pro Tip**: Check local event calendars before your trip to plan your visit around the city's cultural celebrations.

Nearby Attractions

- **The Sarawak State Museum**: Located nearby, this museum is one of the best in Malaysia and showcases Sarawak's diverse cultural heritage, including tribal artifacts, traditional costumes, and archaeological finds.
- **The Cat Museum**: A quirky attraction dedicated to the feline love that Kuching is known for, featuring cat-themed exhibits and statues scattered across the city.

Getting There

- **By Foot**: The **Kuching Waterfront** is located in the heart of the city, making it easily accessible on foot.
- **By Taxi**: Taxis are readily available throughout Kuching and can drop you at the entrance to Fort Margherita or the waterfront.
- **By Boat**: Hop on a traditional **sampan boat** from the waterfront to cross the **Sarawak River** to Fort Margherita, providing a unique and scenic way to reach the fort.

A visit to the **Kuching Waterfront** and **Fort Margherita** is a delightful way to experience Kuching's charm, blending natural beauty with deep cultural and historical significance. Whether you're interested in taking a scenic river cruise, indulging in delicious street food, or exploring the fascinating history of Sarawak, this area offers something for every traveler. Enjoy a leisurely evening by the river, immerse yourself in the vibrant atmosphere, and let the rich heritage of the city inspire you.

Tunku Abdul Rahman Marine Park: A Coastal Paradise in Sabah

Nestled just off the coast of **Kota Kinabalu**, **Tunku Abdul Rahman Marine Park** is a jewel of Sabah, Malaysia, offering pristine beaches, crystal-clear waters, and vibrant marine life. Comprising five stunning islands—**Gaya Island, Manukan Island, Sapi Island, Sulug Island**, and **Pangkor Island**—this marine park is a haven for those seeking a tropical retreat, water activities, and underwater exploration. Whether you're an adventure seeker, a beach lover, or a family on holiday, Tunku Abdul Rahman offers something for everyone.

Why Visit Tunku Abdul Rahman Marine Park?

1. An Ideal Destination for Beach Lovers and Snorkelers

The park's islands boast **white-sand beaches**, **lush tropical landscapes**, and **crystal-clear waters**, making them ideal for relaxation and water sports. The coral reefs surrounding the islands are teeming with vibrant marine life, making it a paradise for snorkelers and divers.

2. Accessible and Close to Kota Kinabalu

Just a short boat ride from **Kota Kinabalu**, the marine park is easy to access for day trips, offering a quick escape from the city's bustling atmosphere to the tranquil beauty of nature.

Highlights of Tunku Abdul Rahman Marine Park

1. Snorkeling and Diving Adventures

- **Coral Reefs and Marine Life**: The marine park is renowned for its healthy and thriving coral reefs, which are home to a variety of marine species, including **clownfish**, **parrotfish**, **turtles**, and even the occasional **blacktip reef shark**. Snorkelers and divers will be treated to an underwater wonderland, where vibrant coral gardens await exploration.
- **Sipadan Island**: If you're an avid diver, **Sipadan Island** is one of the world's top diving destinations, known for its **exceptional biodiversity**. You can expect to see **schools of barracuda**, **turtles**, and **manta rays**, making it a bucket-list destination for diving enthusiasts.
- **Manukan Island**: For beginner divers or those looking to snorkel, **Manukan Island** is perfect. Its shallow waters and clear visibility make it a great spot to explore marine life up close.

2. Relaxation on Pristine Beaches

- **Gaya Island** offers a serene retreat for those seeking relaxation. Its untouched beaches are perfect for lounging by the sea or enjoying a picnic under the shade of palm trees.
- **Sapi Island** is another stunning island with soft sand beaches and turquoise waters, ideal for a peaceful day of sunbathing or swimming.
- **Pro Tip**: Pack sunscreen, water shoes, and a hat to protect yourself from the tropical sun while you relax on the beaches.

3. Water Sports and Outdoor Activities

- **Kayaking and Canoeing**: Kayaks are available for rent on all the islands, providing the perfect opportunity for a leisurely paddle around the coastline and into hidden coves.
- **Jet Skiing and Parasailing**: If you're after more adventure, several of the islands offer thrilling water sports like **jet skiing** and **parasailing**, where you can enjoy the park's beauty from the water and above.
- **Pro Tip**: Bring a waterproof camera or GoPro to capture the exciting moments and marine life during your water sports adventures.

4. Family-Friendly Activities

- **Manukan Island** is particularly suitable for families, with its calm, shallow waters and easy-to-navigate snorkeling spots. Children can explore the vibrant coral gardens and enjoy a safe and educational introduction to marine life.
- The islands also offer **barbecue facilities**, picnic areas, and walking trails, making it perfect for family picnics or a relaxed day on the islands.
- **Pro Tip**: Book a family-friendly tour to ensure that you visit the islands with the best facilities and activities for children.

Pro Tips for Visiting Tunku Abdul Rahman Marine Park

1. Choose the Right Island for Your Interests

- **Manukan Island**: Ideal for families, casual snorkelers, and those who want a range of activities like **beach volleyball**, **picnicking**, and **snorkeling** in shallow waters.
- **Sipadan Island**: Perfect for **experienced divers** seeking world-class diving experiences with diverse marine species, including **pelagic fish**, **reef sharks**, and **coral walls**.
- **Gaya Island**: A great option for those seeking a more secluded, peaceful retreat with minimal crowds, where you can enjoy nature hikes and beach time.
- **Pro Tip**: Check the weather and sea conditions before booking your tour, as some islands are more suitable for certain activities depending on the season.

2. Time Your Visit Wisely

- The best time to visit Tunku Abdul Rahman Marine Park is during the **dry season** (April to October), when the weather is most favorable for water activities and beach relaxation.
- Avoid visiting during **monsoon season** (November to March) as rough seas may affect boat rides and water visibility.
- **Pro Tip**: Weekdays are less crowded than weekends, offering a more tranquil experience. If you can, visit during the week to avoid the crowds and enjoy a peaceful escape.

3. Plan Your Day Trip

- **Day Tours**: Most tours to Tunku Abdul Rahman Islands are day trips that typically start in the morning and end in the late afternoon. If you plan to visit multiple islands, consider booking a **multi-island tour** to get the most out of your day.

- **Pro Tip**: Bring a **dry bag** to keep your personal belongings safe and dry while you enjoy the water and outdoor activities.

4. Stay Safe While Enjoying the Marine Life

- **Snorkeling and Diving**: Always follow the safety guidelines provided by the tour operators and never snorkel or dive alone.
- **Marine Life Respect**: While exploring the underwater world, avoid touching the coral or disturbing the wildlife. Be mindful of your surroundings and leave only footprints behind.
- **Pro Tip**: Bring **reef-safe sunscreen** to protect your skin without harming the coral reefs.

Getting There

- **From Kota Kinabalu**:
    - **By Boat**: The islands are easily accessible by boat from **Kota Kinabalu Marina**. Regular boat services depart in the morning, and the journey takes around **15–30 minutes**, depending on which island you are visiting.
    - **By Car**: Take a **taxi** or private car to the marina, located about **15 minutes** from the city center.
    - **Pro Tip**: Make sure to arrive early to secure your spot on the boat, especially during peak tourist seasons.

Tunku Abdul Rahman Marine Park is a breathtaking destination that offers visitors the perfect blend of adventure, relaxation, and natural beauty. Whether you're diving in crystal-clear waters, enjoying a day on the beach with family, or seeking an adrenaline rush with water sports, the park's five islands have something to offer every type of traveler. Surrounded by stunning coral reefs and pristine marine ecosystems, it's a must-visit for nature lovers, divers, and beach enthusiasts looking to experience the best of Borneo's coastal paradise.

Niah Caves: A Journey Through Time in Sarawak

Tucked within the heart of **Sarawak**, **Niah Caves** is a captivating destination that seamlessly blends **natural beauty** with **archaeological wonder**. Recognized as one of the most significant prehistoric sites in **Southeast Asia**, these caves have revealed **some of the oldest human remains** in the region, offering a unique glimpse into the past. The **Niah Caves** complex, located within the **Niah National Park**, is not just a place to explore geological formations but also a site that traces the footsteps of early human civilizations.

Why Visit Niah Caves?

1. A Historical and Archaeological Treasure

Niah Caves holds profound **archaeological significance**, with human habitation dating back to **40,000 years ago**. The discovery of **prehistoric rock paintings** and ancient **tools** provides invaluable insights into the lives of early humans who lived in the region long before recorded history.

The **Painted Cave**, one of the main attractions, is home to **ancient rock paintings**, some believed to depict scenes from early human rituals and hunting expeditions. It is also the site where **the remains of the oldest known human in Malaysia** were found, adding an extra layer of intrigue and wonder to the experience. For history buffs and archaeology enthusiasts, this site is a must-visit.

2. Explore Dense Rainforest and Limestone Formations

The **Niah Caves** complex is set amidst the lush greenery of the **Sarawak rainforest**, making it a perfect blend of natural beauty and history. The caves themselves are formed from **limestone**, creating stunning stalactites, stalagmites, and eerie passages to explore.

A trek through the surrounding rainforest takes visitors on an immersive journey through tropical biodiversity, where you may encounter a variety of wildlife and plant species endemic to the area. The experience is not only educational but offers a chance to connect with nature in its most primitive form.

Highlights of Niah Caves

1. Prehistoric Rock Paintings

- The **Painted Cave**, located within the Niah Caves complex, is one of the main highlights. It features **rock paintings** believed to date back thousands of years.

- These paintings include **human figures**, **hand stencils**, and depictions of **animals** and **hunting scenes**, which offer a rare glimpse into the spiritual and daily life of early inhabitants of Borneo.
- **Pro Tip**: Bring a **flashlight** or **headlamp** to properly view the paintings inside the caves, as some areas may be dimly lit.

2. Niah Cave's Archaeological Significance

- The **Large Cave** is where the discovery of **human remains** and ancient artifacts took place. Archaeologists have uncovered evidence of a settlement dating back to the **Late Pleistocene** era, adding to the caves' importance as a critical archaeological site.
- In the cave, you can see **excavation sites** where the remains of early humans were found along with burial offerings, creating a vivid historical context.
- **Pro Tip**: Hiring a **local guide** is essential to fully grasp the historical significance of these discoveries. They provide insightful information about the cave's role in the prehistory of Southeast Asia.

3. Trek Through Dense Rainforest

- The entrance to Niah Caves is a **short trek through dense rainforest**, which adds a sense of adventure and anticipation before reaching the caves themselves. Along the way, keep your eyes peeled for local wildlife, including **monkeys**, **birds**, and **insects**.
- The journey through the forest is both enriching and scenic, with tropical foliage and an abundance of natural life.
- **Pro Tip**: Wear **comfortable shoes** with good grip and **long-sleeve clothing** to protect yourself from potential insect bites as you make your way through the rainforest.

4. The "Human Remains" Exhibit

- Niah Caves is home to a small museum that exhibits the **human remains** and **artifacts** discovered within the caves. This is a great opportunity to further understand the archaeological findings and their significance.
- The museum provides information on the **excavation process**, the **methods** used by archaeologists, and how the findings have changed our understanding of early human life in Borneo.
- **Pro Tip**: Take some time to explore the museum after your cave visit to deepen your understanding of the site's historical context.

Pro Tips for Visiting Niah Caves

1. Hiring a Guide

- To fully appreciate the archaeological importance of Niah Caves, it's highly recommended to hire a **local guide**. Guides offer invaluable knowledge about the cave's **prehistory**, the rock paintings, and the **discovery of human remains**, bringing the experience to life.
- Guides also help navigate the cave systems and ensure that you safely explore the cave's hidden nooks.
- **Pro Tip**: You can hire a guide directly at the entrance of Niah National Park or pre-book through local tour agencies.

2. Wear Comfortable and Practical Clothing

- The **trek to the caves** involves a moderate walk through the rainforest and within the cave itself, which can be wet and slippery. Wear **sturdy hiking boots** or **closed-toed shoes** with a good grip to avoid slipping.
- **Bring a light jacket** or **rain poncho** in case of unpredictable weather and ensure you have plenty of **water** for hydration.

3. Be Prepared for Cave Exploration

- Niah Caves are **partially lit**, but some areas require a **flashlight** or **headlamp** for better visibility. Make sure you have a **reliable flashlight** with extra batteries for exploring the inner cave passages.
- The air inside can be **humid**, so dress appropriately and wear **light, breathable clothing** for comfort.

4. Respect the Site

- As Niah Caves is an important archaeological site, it's essential to respect the **preservation rules**. Do not touch or disturb the rock paintings, human remains, or any artifacts you may encounter during your visit.
- Be mindful of your **footprints** and try to leave the site as you found it to ensure future generations can enjoy the caves in the same pristine state.
- **Pro Tip**: Bring a **camera** but be mindful of flash photography in sensitive areas, as it can damage ancient artworks.

Getting There

- **From Miri**:
    - **By Car**: Niah Caves is located about **70 kilometers** from **Miri**, which is approximately **1.5 hours by car**. You can take a taxi or rent a car for the drive.
    - **By Bus**: Local buses from Miri to **Niah National Park** are available, but they may be infrequent, so it's recommended to check schedules in advance.
    - **Pro Tip**: Arrange a **private transport** or **hire a local driver** to ensure a seamless trip, especially if you are unfamiliar with the area.

Niah Caves is not just an incredible natural wonder, but a **gateway to understanding the deep history** of Southeast Asia and the early human settlements of Borneo. For those interested in **archaeology, cultural heritage**, and **natural exploration**, a visit to Niah Caves is an unforgettable journey back in time. With its prehistoric rock art, ancient remains, and fascinating cave systems, Niah Caves offers a unique blend of adventure and education that is a must for any history lover visiting **Sarawak**.

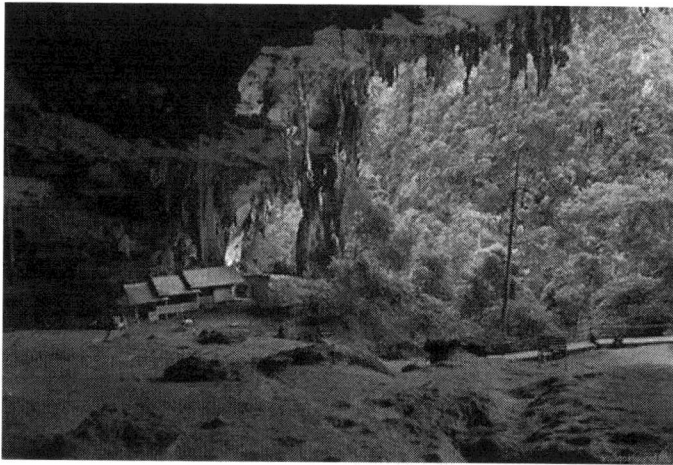

Poring Hot Springs and Canopy Walkway: A Refreshing Escape in Sabah

Located in the serene foothills of **Mount Kinabalu**, **Poring Hot Springs** is a perfect blend of relaxation and adventure. Known for its rejuvenating **thermal pools**, the area also offers a variety of natural attractions, including a stunning **canopy walkway**, lush butterfly gardens, and the rare opportunity to witness the **Rafflesia flower**, one of the world's largest blooms. Whether you're looking to unwind in the healing waters or explore Borneo's rich biodiversity, Poring provides an experience that caters to every type of traveler.

Why Visit Poring Hot Springs and Canopy Walkway?

1. Thermal Pools for Relaxation

- The highlight of **Poring Hot Springs** is the **thermal sulfur pools** that are believed to have healing properties. These naturally warm waters are perfect for soothing sore muscles and rejuvenating the body after a trek or long journey.
- The **hot springs** have both public and private pools, giving visitors the option for a more secluded experience. The pools are set amidst the lush greenery of the **Kinabalu Park**, offering a peaceful and calming atmosphere.
- **Pro Tip**: **Arrive early** to avoid the midday crowds, particularly if you prefer a quiet, more tranquil experience. **Bring swimwear** and a towel, as these are required for the thermal baths.

2. Canopy Walkway for a Bird's-Eye View

- The **Poring Canopy Walkway** is a thrilling **treetop walk** suspended 40 meters above the forest floor, offering breathtaking views of the surrounding rainforest and the majestic **Mount Kinabalu**.
- This **1.2-kilometer-long walkway** is an exhilarating experience for nature lovers and adventure seekers. As you traverse through the treetops, you'll be able to spot a variety of **wildlife** and observe the vibrant ecosystems that thrive in this unique environment.
- **Pro Tip**: The **canopy walk** can be a bit challenging for those with a fear of heights, so take your time and enjoy the view at your

own pace. Don't forget to wear **comfortable shoes** for the short trek to the walkway's starting point.

3. Butterfly Garden: A Colorful Escape

- Poring is home to a **butterfly garden** that boasts a variety of colorful species, many of which are endemic to Borneo. The garden is a peaceful spot where visitors can marvel at the vibrant **butterflies** and learn more about the important role they play in the ecosystem.
- The garden's **well-maintained trails** allow you to observe these delicate creatures up close, making it a fantastic stop for photographers and nature enthusiasts.
- **Pro Tip**: Visit the butterfly garden in the **early morning** when the butterflies are most active. Bring a **camera** with a **macro lens** for capturing intricate close-ups.

4. Rafflesia Flower Sightings

- **Poring Hot Springs** is one of the best places in Borneo to witness the blooming of the **Rafflesia flower**, the world's largest single flower. The flower, which can grow up to **one meter in diameter**, is famous for its distinct smell, often likened to rotting flesh, which attracts its pollinators—**carrion beetles**.
- The rare and stunning **Rafflesia** typically blooms for just **7 to 9 days**, making it a **seasonal attraction**. Its bloom is a breathtaking sight and an unforgettable experience for nature lovers.
- **Pro Tip**: The blooming of the Rafflesia is unpredictable, so **check with the park rangers** for sightings and try to time your visit when the flower is in bloom. Be prepared to venture into the jungle for a bit of a hike if you're seeking out one of these rare flowers.

Highlights of Poring Hot Springs and Canopy Walkway

1. Thermal Pools and Natural Hot Springs

- Soak in the healing **sulfuric waters** of the thermal pools, which are said to provide relief from **muscle pain**, **joint stiffness**, and other ailments. The hot springs' therapeutic properties make them an essential part of the Poring experience.
- **Private pools** are available for those seeking more seclusion, while **public pools** allow for a more social experience.
- **Pro Tip**: If you're visiting on a **weekend**, consider booking your private pool in advance, as they can fill up quickly.

2. Canopy Walkway for a Thrilling Treetop Experience

- Walk above the treetops and see the rainforest from an entirely new perspective. The canopy walkway is the ideal way to explore the rich biodiversity of the area while keeping your feet dry.
- With its **high vantage point**, it's an excellent place for **birdwatching**—you might spot species such as the **hornbill** and **orange-bellied flowerpecker**.
- **Pro Tip**: The **canopy walkway** can sway slightly, so be prepared for a gentle rocking motion as you walk across. Take your time and enjoy the panoramic views.

3. Rafflesia and Other Flora and Fauna

- The region around **Poring** is rich in **biodiversity**, home to a variety of **plants**, **wildlife**, and rare flowers like the **Rafflesia**.
- You can explore the surrounding **rainforest trails** to discover exotic plant species, **wild orchids**, and unique fungi.
- **Pro Tip**: If you're keen to see the **Rafflesia**, plan your trip between **March and June** when the blooms are most likely. However, the flowers are elusive, so **consult with local rangers** for bloom forecasts.

Practical Information and Tips for Visiting Poring Hot Springs

1. Getting There

- **From Kota Kinabalu**: Poring Hot Springs is approximately **2 hours' drive** from **Kota Kinabalu** (around 110 km). You can hire a **private taxi**, rent a car, or join a guided tour.
- **By Public Transport**: You can take a **bus** from **Kota Kinabalu** to **Kinabalu Park**, and from there, catch a **local taxi** or shuttle to **Poring Hot Springs**.
- **Pro Tip**: If you're short on time, consider booking a **private tour** that includes transport, entry, and a guide to make the most of your visit.

2. Entry Fees

- There is an entry fee for **Kinabalu Park** and Poring Hot Springs. The fees are generally modest, but it's important to check the latest rates upon arrival.
- **Pro Tip**: Keep your **receipt** handy when entering as it will be required for entry to the hot springs and the canopy walkway.

3. Accommodation Options

- Poring Hot Springs has a range of accommodation options, from **basic lodges** and **guesthouses** to **resorts**. If you want to immerse yourself in the natural surroundings, consider staying at the **Poring Hot Springs Resort**, which offers **private hot spring baths** for guests.

- For a more **rustic experience**, there are also nearby **camping grounds** available for those who prefer to sleep under the stars.
- **Pro Tip**: Book your accommodation in advance, especially during peak seasons (weekends and public holidays), as Poring can get busy.

Poring Hot Springs and its surrounding attractions offer a unique opportunity to experience the natural beauty and healing properties of Borneo. Whether you're soaking in the therapeutic waters, exploring the treetops on the canopy walkway, or witnessing the rare and majestic **Rafflesia flower**, Poring is an unforgettable destination. Ideal for nature lovers, adventure seekers, and those simply looking to relax, **Poring Hot Springs** offers a little bit of everything—making it an essential stop on your journey through **Sabah**.

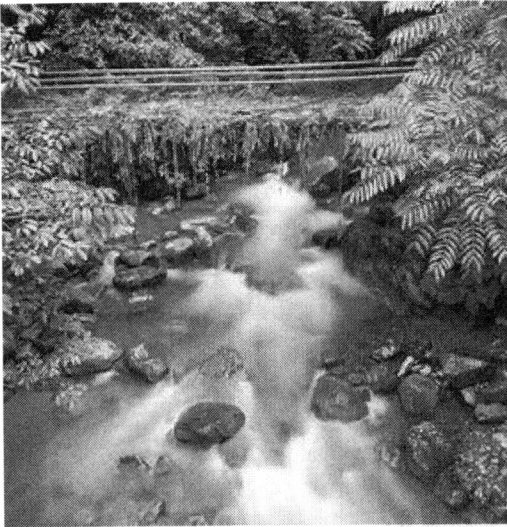

Chapter 7

Suggestions for Travelers: Additional Hidden Gems in Borneo

For those with extra time to explore beyond the must-visit landmarks, Borneo has even more incredible destinations that offer a deeper look into its diverse ecosystems, fascinating history, and vibrant culture. Here are three bonus suggestions that should definitely make your travel itinerary if you're craving more adventure.

1. Bako National Park (Sarawak, Malaysia)

Located just a short drive from **Kuching, Bako National Park** is one of the oldest and most visited parks in **Sarawak**, known for its extraordinary array of ecosystems and wildlife. Despite its compact size, Bako offers a remarkable variety of habitats, from mangrove swamps to dipterocarp forests and **sandstone cliffs**.

- **Wildlife Spotting**: This park is famous for its resident **proboscis monkeys**, the unique primate species with their distinct, large noses. Bako also hosts other fascinating wildlife such as **long-tailed macaques**, **silver-leaf monkeys**, and a plethora of bird species, making it a great destination for **wildlife photographers** and **birdwatchers**.
- **Hiking Trails**: The park offers several well-maintained **hiking trails** of varying difficulty, allowing visitors to experience the jungle up close. Popular trails include the **Teluk Paku** and **Tanjung Sapi** paths, where hikers can enjoy stunning views of the **South China Sea** and explore the park's diverse habitats.
- **Pro Tip**: The best way to reach Bako is by taking a **taxi** or **public transport** from **Kuching**, followed by a short boat ride. **Arrive**

early to maximize your time for wildlife spotting, especially the **proboscis monkeys** at dawn.

---

2. Lambir Hills National Park (Sarawak, Malaysia)

A true haven for hiking and nature enthusiasts, **Lambir Hills National Park** is a lesser-known gem in **Sarawak** that offers stunning trails, rich biodiversity, and picturesque **waterfalls**. The park is known for its **tropical rainforests**, which are home to a variety of plants and animals, many of which are rare or endangered.

- **Waterfalls and Hikes**: Visitors can hike along the park's well-marked **trails** to discover waterfalls like **Latak Waterfall** and **Pantu Waterfall**, where crystal-clear waters cascade into cool pools—perfect for a refreshing dip after a hike. Some trails are relatively easy, while others can be more challenging, taking adventurers deeper into the forest to explore hidden **flora** and **fauna**.
- **Wildlife**: Lambir Hills is also home to a wealth of wildlife, including the **sunda pangolin**, **wild boars**, **hornbills**, and various species of **insects** and **butterflies**. It's an excellent destination for those who want to experience Borneo's natural biodiversity away from the crowds.
- **Pro Tip**: Wear **lightweight, moisture-wicking clothing** and sturdy **hiking boots** to make the most of your visit. If you're interested in swimming at the waterfalls, bring a towel and swimwear, and ensure you're cautious of strong currents.

---

3. Labuan Island (Malaysia)

A short hop from **Kota Kinabalu**, **Labuan Island** is a small, serene territory with a fascinating mix of history, duty-free shopping, and

114

beautiful beaches. Known for its significance during **World War II**, Labuan is also a relaxing place for those seeking a quiet retreat after exploring the wild jungles of Borneo.

- **World War II History**: Labuan was the site of intense fighting during World War II, and it remains home to several significant historical landmarks, including the **Labuan War Cemetery**, which honors the Australian soldiers who lost their lives in the battle for Borneo. History buffs will appreciate the **World War II Memorial**, as well as **Surrender Point**, where Japanese forces officially surrendered to the Allies in 1945.
- **Duty-Free Shopping**: Labuan Island is a **duty-free zone**, making it a popular spot for those looking to purchase luxury goods at significantly lower prices. From **alcohol** to **cigarettes**, **cosmetics**, and **chocolates**, you'll find great deals in the shopping malls and local markets.
- **Beaches and Water Activities**: Labuan's coastal areas are home to some of Borneo's most tranquil beaches. Visitors can enjoy activities such as **snorkeling**, **diving**, and **swimming** in the crystal-clear waters, or simply relax on the **white sand beaches**. For underwater enthusiasts, the island also has several **wreck dives**, including the **American F4F Wildcat aircraft wreck**, which provides an interesting glimpse into the island's wartime past.
- **Pro Tip**: Labuan Island is best explored at a **relaxed pace**. If you're keen to experience the duty-free shopping, visit **Labuan International Bazaar** or **Financial Park** for the best selection of goods. For beachgoers, **Tanjung Aru Beach** is a beautiful place to unwind and enjoy the calm waters.

Incorporating these bonus destinations into your itinerary will only enhance your experience of Borneo, a place where nature, culture, and history come together in the most remarkable ways. Whether you're seeking wildlife encounters in the dense jungles of **Bako** and **Lambir Hills**, uncovering the war-torn history of **Labuan**, or relaxing by some of the island's pristine beaches, these additional locations offer a deeper connection to Borneo's heart.

These **hidden gems**, along with the **top ten landmarks** already mentioned, will create a **diverse and unforgettable journey** across this extraordinary island. **Borneo** is not just a destination; it's an adventure, an exploration of uncharted territories, and a celebration of the earth's natural and cultural treasures.

Cultural and Historical Gems

Borneo is a land rich in cultural heritage and historical significance. The diverse indigenous communities, colonial influences, and royal traditions have shaped the region's unique identity. Among its most remarkable cultural and historical landmarks, **Sarawak Cultural Village** and **Istana Nurul Iman** stand out as must-visit locations for travelers eager to explore the island's heritage.

Sarawak Cultural Village: A Living Museum

Located just outside **Kuching**, at the foot of **Mount Santubong**, the **Sarawak Cultural Village** is a living museum that showcases the heritage and customs of Sarawak's various indigenous groups. This open-air museum is one of the best places to immerse yourself in the traditional lifestyles of the **Iban**, **Bidayuh**, **Orang Ulu**, **Melanau**, and other indigenous tribes of Sarawak. The village functions as a cultural center, where visitors can explore longhouses, experience local rituals, and observe the customs that have been passed down for centuries.

- **Highlights**:
  - **Traditional Longhouses**: Each tribe has a distinct longhouse that reflects their way of life. The **Iban longhouse** offers insight into their rice farming and

116

headhunting traditions, while the **Orang Ulu's longhouse** showcases intricate beadwork and carvings.

- ○ **Cultural Performances**: The village hosts regular performances where dancers, musicians, and storytellers engage visitors in traditional arts. Be sure to watch a **Sape** performance (a traditional instrument) and see the **Bidayuh dance**—both are mesmerizing examples of Sarawak's artistic legacy.
- ○ **Craftsmanship and Workshops**: You can try your hand at traditional crafts, such as **weaving**, **batik painting**, and **beadwork**, often guided by local artisans.
- ○ **Festival of Culture**: If you're fortunate enough to visit during the **Festival of Cultures**, you'll witness an explosion of color, music, and dance that celebrates the diversity of Sarawak's ethnic groups.

- **Pro Tip**: Visit the village in the **morning** when it is quieter, allowing you more time to explore the exhibits and interact with the locals without crowds. The **cultural performances** are typically held in the afternoon, so plan accordingly to ensure you don't miss them.

- **Why Visit**: The **Sarawak Cultural Village** is not just a museum; it is a vibrant, living showcase of the indigenous cultures of Sarawak. It provides an incredible opportunity to learn about and experience firsthand the traditions and daily life of Borneo's indigenous peoples, making it a must-visit destination for anyone interested in the cultural heart of Borneo.

Istana Nurul Iman: The World's Largest Residential Palace

Situated along the **Brunei River** in **Bandar Seri Begawan**, **Istana Nurul Iman** is the official residence of the Sultan of Brunei and is recognized as the world's largest residential palace. With its sprawling compound and opulent design, it is a symbol of Brunei's royal heritage, wealth, and Islamic traditions. The palace serves not only as the Sultan's home but also as the center of government and national ceremonies.

- **Highlights**:

    o **Architectural Grandeur**: **Istana Nurul Iman** is a modern masterpiece of Islamic architecture. Its **golden domes** and **marble facades** reflect the Sultan's wealth and Brunei's commitment to Islamic art. The palace contains **1,788 rooms, 257 bathrooms, and 5 swimming pools**—a testament to its sheer scale and opulence.

    o **The Royal Grounds**: While the palace itself is not open to the public on a daily basis, the surrounding **gardens** and the **ceremonial barge** on the **Brunei River** offer visitors a chance to marvel at the beauty of the complex. During special events like **Hari Raya (Eid al-Fitr)**, the Sultan and royal family host an open house, offering a rare chance to enter the palace and witness its splendor firsthand.

    o **Royal Ceremonies**: The palace is the site of several key national events, including the Sultan's birthday celebrations and religious festivals. These events are an important part of Brunei's political and cultural life, often broadcast for the public.

    o **Pro Tip**: Although the palace itself is closed to tourists, a **visit during the Sultan's birthday** or **Hari Raya** celebrations is a great opportunity to witness the palace's grandeur in a live setting. Make sure to arrive early to avoid the crowds, and be prepared to dress appropriately for the occasion.

- **Why Visit**: **Istana Nurul Iman** is not just a palace; it is a living symbol of **Brunei's monarchy** and **Islamic culture**. The sheer scale and beauty of the palace, combined with the unique chance to experience Brunei's royal ceremonies, make this a must-visit for those interested in exploring the lavish heritage of this tiny yet wealthy nation.

Both **Sarawak Cultural Village** and **Istana Nurul Iman** represent the deep cultural roots and the historical significance of Borneo. **Sarawak Cultural Village** offers an immersive experience into the rich traditions of Sarawak's indigenous people, while **Istana Nurul Iman** showcases the grandeur and elegance of Brunei's monarchy. These cultural and historical landmarks are essential for anyone looking to understand the soul of Borneo, offering a perfect blend of local history, art, and royal heritage that highlights the diversity and depth of this remarkable island.

A visit to these places will leave you with lasting memories of Borneo's fascinating cultural mosaic, where every tradition and royal relic tells a story of its own.

Fort Margherita: Colonial Echoes in Kuching

Overlooking the serene **Sarawak River** in **Kuching**, **Fort Margherita** stands as a reminder of the region's colonial past, blending history with captivating views. Built in 1879 by the second **Rajah Brooke, Charles Brooke**, the fort was originally intended to protect Kuching from pirate attacks, as well as to uphold British control over the region. Today, it serves as a museum that tells the story of Sarawak's colonial era and its transition into modernity.

- **Highlights**:
  - **The Brooke Era Exhibits**: The fort's museum is dedicated to the history of the **Rajah Brooke dynasty**, the British colonial rulers who governed Sarawak for over a century. Inside, you'll find a collection of old photographs, artifacts, and stories that chronicle the era's impact on Sarawak's development, from the arrival of the Brooke family to the eventual independence of the state.
  - **Breathtaking Views**: Perched on a hill, the fort offers panoramic views of **Kuching** and the **Sarawak River**. It's a great spot to snap pictures of the city's skyline and the surrounding landscape, providing a peaceful and picturesque setting for reflection.
  - **Fort Architecture**: The architecture of **Fort Margherita** remains mostly intact, with its **high walls**, **watchtowers**, and **cannon emplacements** reminiscent of a bygone era. It's one of the best-preserved examples of colonial military architecture in the region.
  - **River Cruise Access**: A **riverboat cruise** to the fort from Kuching's waterfront is a relaxing and scenic way to reach the location, allowing you to enjoy the beauty of the river and its surrounding landscapes.
- **Pro Tip**: Visit **Fort Margherita** in the **late afternoon** when the crowds are fewer, and you can enjoy the sunset views over Kuching and the river. The nearby **Brooke Gallery** in **Kuching's waterfront** provides additional historical insights into the legacy of the Brooke family.

- **Why Visit**: **Fort Margherita** is an essential visit for those interested in the colonial history of Borneo, offering an intimate glimpse into Sarawak's past. The fort's serene location and engaging exhibitions make it an ideal destination for history buffs and anyone looking to understand the complex historical narrative of Kuching.

Longhouses of the Dayak Tribes: Traditional Community Living

In the heart of Borneo, the **longhouses** of the **Dayak tribes** represent one of the island's most enduring and unique cultural traditions. The Dayaks, Borneo's indigenous peoples, have lived in communal longhouses for centuries. These longhouses, often stretching over 100 meters in length, are a testament to the Dayak way of life—rooted in strong communal ties, spiritual practices, and nature-based subsistence living.

- **Highlights**:

  - **Traditional Architecture**: The longhouses are impressive structures, built from wood and bamboo, with high thatched roofs designed to withstand the humid tropical climate. Each longhouse can accommodate multiple families, with separate living spaces for each household, but shared communal areas for dining and socializing. The architecture is an expression of the **Dayak's deep connection to nature** and community-oriented lifestyle.
  - **Cultural Insight**: Visiting a Dayak longhouse provides insight into the **spiritual beliefs, daily activities**, and **rituals** of the Dayak tribes. You'll often see traditional **weaving, wood carving**, and **beadwork** on display, as well as participate in communal activities like dancing, music, and feasts.
  - **Meet the Dayak People**: Most visits to longhouses include opportunities to meet the inhabitants, who are often eager to share their stories, offer you a taste of their local food, and invite you into their way of life. The experience provides a rare chance to interact with a

traditional society that has remained largely unchanged by modern influences.

- o **Jungle Surroundings**: Many Dayak longhouses are situated deep in the heart of Borneo's rainforests, with **dense jungle** and **flowing rivers** surrounding them. The natural beauty adds another layer of intrigue to the visit, with the sounds of the jungle serving as a background to the lifestyle that has existed for centuries.
- **Pro Tip**: While visiting Dayak longhouses, respect local customs and ask for permission before taking photographs, especially of people and their sacred rituals. Bring a **good pair of hiking shoes** if you plan to trek through the jungle to reach a longhouse.

- **Why Visit**: The **longhouses of the Dayak tribes** offer a profound cultural experience, allowing you to step back in time and witness an ancient way of life that is rapidly disappearing. Visiting these communities is a rare opportunity to engage directly with Borneo's indigenous cultures, preserving their customs and traditions while supporting their local economies.

Both **Fort Margherita** and the **Dayak longhouses** are essential destinations for anyone interested in understanding Borneo's complex cultural and historical landscape. **Fort Margherita** offers a look at the colonial influences that shaped modern-day **Kuching**, while the **longhouses** of the **Dayak tribes** provide a window into the indigenous traditions and communal life that have existed for millennia. Together, these landmarks offer a rich tapestry of Borneo's diverse cultural heritage, making them indispensable stops on your journey through this extraordinary island.

Kota Kinabalu Waterfront: A Modern Hub by the Sea

Kota Kinabalu, the capital city of **Sabah**, has long been known for its stunning natural beauty and vibrant cultural heritage. However, in recent years, the **Kota Kinabalu Waterfront** has emerged as a modern urban oasis, offering visitors a blend of luxury shopping, dining, entertainment, and stunning views of the South China Sea and nearby islands.

- **Highlights**:

  - **Waterfront Promenade**: The waterfront promenade is a **picturesque pathway** that stretches along the coastline, perfect for a leisurely stroll while soaking in the views of the bustling city skyline on one side and the tranquil sea on the other. As the sun sets, the waterfront comes alive with vibrant colors, creating a spectacular backdrop for evening activities.

  - **Dining and Shopping**: The area boasts a range of **high-end restaurants, cafes,** and **bars** offering both local Bornean and international cuisine. Seafood lovers will delight in the fresh catches from the surrounding seas. The **Suria Sabah Shopping Mall**, located nearby, provides upscale shopping options and entertainment facilities, including a cinema and arcades.

  - **Sailing and Cruises**: For those seeking adventure, the waterfront is also a hub for **boat tours** and **sailing cruises**, offering visitors the chance to explore the nearby islands such as **Manukan** and **Sapi** in the **Tunku Abdul Rahman Marine Park**. These trips provide an exciting escape from the city, allowing you to snorkel, dive, or simply relax on pristine beaches.

  - **Cultural Influences**: The waterfront area is also a reflection of the city's unique mix of cultures. While enjoying the modern amenities, visitors can also experience the rich history and heritage of **Kota Kinabalu**, from the **Chinese temples** to the **Filipino market** where local artisans sell traditional handicrafts.

- **Pro Tip**: If you're visiting in the evening, make sure to grab a seat at one of the waterfront cafes to witness the **breathtaking**

sunset over the sea, or perhaps even indulge in **happy hour** at a rooftop bar while taking in the panoramic views.

- **Why Visit**: The **Kota Kinabalu Waterfront** represents a fusion of modern urban life and natural beauty, offering something for everyone—from food lovers and shopaholics to nature enthusiasts. Its central location makes it an ideal spot for visitors to relax, unwind, and experience the cosmopolitan vibe of Kota Kinabalu, while still being surrounded by the majestic beauty of Borneo's coastline.

Bandar Seri Begawan's Omar Ali Saifuddien Mosque: The Jewel of Brunei

Omar Ali Saifuddien Mosque, located in **Bandar Seri Begawan**, the capital of **Brunei**, is one of the most iconic landmarks in Southeast Asia, epitomizing the country's wealth, Islamic heritage, and architectural grandeur. Completed in 1958 and named after the 28th Sultan of Brunei, **Sultan Omar Ali Saifuddien**, the mosque is not only a place of worship but also a cultural symbol and a testament to the nation's devotion to Islam.

- **Highlights**:

  - **Golden Dome and Minarets**: The mosque's centerpiece is its **golden dome**, which glistens under the tropical sun, making it a standout feature on the Brunei skyline. The **minarets** rise elegantly into the sky, complementing the grand design of the building. The mosque's design merges **Moorish**, **Italian Renaissance**, and **Malay** architectural styles, creating a stunning visual fusion.
  - **The Serene Lagoon**: The mosque is surrounded by a tranquil **man-made lagoon**, which enhances its ethereal

beauty. The lagoon reflects the mosque's impressive façade, creating a **stunning photographic opportunity**, especially at dusk when the mosque lights up against the darkening sky. This serene setting makes it one of the most photographed sites in Brunei.

- o **The Interior**: Inside the mosque, visitors will be mesmerized by the **intricate marble floors, carved teakwood panels**, and **beautiful stained glass windows**. The mosque's interior is equally lavish, with a spacious prayer hall capable of accommodating thousands of worshippers. The intricate details and serene atmosphere inside the mosque create an awe-inspiring spiritual experience.

- o **Ceremonial Barge**: Adjacent to the mosque is a **ceremonial barge**, which was once used by the Sultan for royal events. This **floating vessel** adds to the grandeur of the mosque complex and offers a glimpse into the royal history and ceremonies of Brunei.

- o **Sultan's Mosque Grounds**: The grounds surrounding the mosque are beautifully landscaped, with lush gardens and peaceful walkways. It's an ideal spot for visitors to enjoy the mosque's beauty from different angles and appreciate the tranquil environment that Brunei is known for.

- **Pro Tip**: The mosque is open to tourists, but visitors should dress modestly and respectfully. Women are required to wear a headscarf, and all visitors should wear long pants or skirts. Visit during the day to catch the mosque's beauty in full daylight, or in the evening to witness the mesmerizing **reflection of the golden dome** in the water.

- **Why Visit**: The **Omar Ali Saifuddien Mosque** is a must-visit landmark for anyone traveling to **Bandar Seri Begawan**. Not only does it showcase Brunei's Islamic architectural brilliance, but it also offers a peaceful and contemplative environment for reflection. Whether you are interested in architecture, history, or simply seeking a tranquil space, this mosque will leave you with a lasting impression of Brunei's cultural and religious identity.

Both the **Kota Kinabalu Waterfront** and **Omar Ali Saifuddien Mosque** are perfect examples of how Borneo balances modern development with deep cultural and historical roots. The **waterfront** provides a lively urban experience with natural beauty, while the mosque offers a sacred and majestic symbol of Brunei's religious and architectural legacy. Each site captures a different facet of the island, from the cosmopolitan charm of **Kota Kinabalu** to the serene grandeur of **Bandar Seri Begawan**, making them essential stops on any Borneo itinerary.

Chapter 8

Suggested Itinerary

Family-Friendly Itinerary (7 Days): Wildlife Parks and Accessible Adventures

Borneo is an ideal destination for families seeking a blend of wildlife encounters, cultural experiences, and natural beauty. With its diverse range of accessible activities, the island offers something for all ages. This **7-day itinerary** focuses on wildlife parks, family-friendly adventures, and comfortable accommodations, ensuring a memorable vacation for the entire family.

Day 1: Arrival in Kota Kinabalu, Sabah

Morning:
Arrive at **Kota Kinabalu International Airport**. Take a leisurely transfer to your hotel, where you can rest and freshen up after your flight.

Afternoon:
After settling in, explore the **Kota Kinabalu Waterfront**. Stroll along the promenade, where you can admire the sunset views and enjoy casual family dining at one of the nearby restaurants. For a cultural touch, visit the **Filipino Market** for unique handicrafts.

Evening:
Dinner at a family-friendly restaurant, such as **D'Place Kinabalu**, which offers a variety of local dishes and a relaxed atmosphere.

Day 2: Visit to Tunku Abdul Rahman Marine Park

Morning:
Take a boat trip to the **Tunku Abdul Rahman Marine Park**, a group of five islands just off the coast of **Kota Kinabalu**. Choose **Manukan Island** for a family-friendly beach day with gentle waters and white sand beaches, ideal for children.

Afternoon:
Relax on the beach, enjoy a picnic, or explore the island's short walking trails. Snorkeling is also available, where children can enjoy observing colorful coral reefs and marine life with a guide.

Evening:
Return to Kota Kinabalu for dinner. Consider dining at **The Seafood Place**, known for its fresh catches and welcoming atmosphere for families.

Day 3: Wildlife at the Sepilok Orangutan Rehabilitation Centre

Morning:
Fly to **Sandakan** (approximately 40-minute flight). Upon arrival, head straight to the **Sepilok Orangutan Rehabilitation Centre**. This world-renowned sanctuary is dedicated to rescuing orphaned and injured orangutans. Watch the feeding session and enjoy observing these magnificent primates up close.

Afternoon:
After the orangutan feeding, take a walk along the **Rainforest Discovery Centre**. The center offers canopy walks, birdwatching opportunities, and a nature trail that is easily accessible for families.

Evening:
Check into your accommodation in **Sandakan** and enjoy a quiet dinner. A recommended family-friendly option is **Sanbay Restaurant**, where you can taste local dishes in a laid-back setting.

Day 4: River Safari along the Kinabatangan River

Morning:
Start your day with a transfer to the **Kinabatangan River** area. Embark on a **river safari** to spot wildlife such as pygmy elephants, orangutans, proboscis monkeys, and an abundance of birdlife. The gentle river cruise is an excellent way for families to enjoy Borneo's biodiversity without too much physical exertion.

Afternoon:
After your river safari, enjoy a family-friendly jungle trek or a guided walk through the surrounding forests to learn about the area's flora and fauna.

Evening:
Spend the night in a **river lodge**, such as the **Kinabatangan River Lodge**, where you can relax and enjoy the peaceful surroundings.

Day 5: Visit to the Bornean Sun Bear Conservation Centre

Morning:
After breakfast, head to the **Bornean Sun Bear Conservation Centre**. This center is dedicated to the protection of the world's smallest bear species, the **sun bear**. Your family can learn about these bears and observe them in a natural, jungle environment.

Afternoon:
Take the afternoon to visit **Labuk Bay Proboscis Monkey Sanctuary**, located nearby, to watch the quirky **proboscis monkeys** feed and interact in their natural habitat.

Evening:
Return to **Sandakan** for a family-friendly dinner at the **Kampung**

129

Nelayan Seafood Restaurant, offering delicious fresh seafood and a beautiful view of the bay.

Day 6: Cultural Exploration and Adventure in Kota Kinabalu

Morning:
Fly back to **Kota Kinabalu** and visit the **Mari Mari Cultural Village** for a fun and educational cultural experience. Here, your family can learn about the traditional lifestyles of Borneo's indigenous tribes through hands-on activities such as traditional cooking and dance performances.

Afternoon:
Take a short trip to **Poring Hot Springs** in the foothills of **Mount Kinabalu**. Enjoy a soak in the therapeutic hot springs and take a gentle **canopy walkway** to see the rainforest from above.

Evening:
Head back to Kota Kinabalu for dinner and a night out at **Kota Kinabalu's Night Market**, where the family can try a variety of local snacks and enjoy the bustling atmosphere.

Day 7: Departure

Morning:
Spend the morning relaxing at the hotel or doing some last-minute shopping at **Suria Sabah Mall**.

Afternoon:
Depending on your flight time, you can enjoy a final stroll along **Kota Kinabalu Waterfront** before transferring to the airport for your departure.

Family-Friendly Tips

- **Accommodations**: Choose family-friendly accommodations with convenient amenities like swimming pools, spacious rooms, and proximity to attractions. In Kota Kinabalu, **Shangri-La's Tanjung Aru Resort & Spa** offers a fantastic family experience with its beachfront location and kid-friendly facilities.
- **Meals**: Opt for restaurants that offer a variety of options for children. Many local restaurants in Borneo serve mild versions of traditional dishes like **laksa** and **nasi lemak**, which are great for younger palates.
- **Transportation**: In Borneo, domestic flights are often the fastest way to cover long distances. For short distances, taxis or private transfers are usually the best way to get around with children. Ensure your chosen accommodations offer shuttle services to nearby attractions for added convenience.

This **7-day family-friendly itinerary** offers a perfect mix of wildlife, culture, and relaxation. It's designed to be easygoing yet enriching, with plenty of opportunities for both adventure and rest, making it an ideal Borneo vacation for families with children of all ages.

Adventure Seekers Itinerary (10 Days): Trekking, Diving, and Thrill-Seeking

Borneo is a paradise for adrenaline junkies, offering some of the best trekking, diving, and wildlife experiences in the world. From scaling the towering peaks of **Mount Kinabalu** to diving in the crystal-clear waters of **Sipadan Island**, this **10-day adventure itinerary** is packed with exhilarating activities that will leave you breathless and craving more. Whether you're a hiker, diver, or nature enthusiast, Borneo's untamed wilderness and stunning landscapes will cater to every thrill-seeking traveler.

Day 1: Arrival in Kota Kinabalu, Sabah

Morning:
Arrive at **Kota Kinabalu International Airport** and take a transfer to your hotel. Rest and prepare for your exciting journey ahead.

Afternoon:
Spend the afternoon exploring **Kota Kinabalu's bustling waterfront**. Enjoy a meal at **The Seafood Place** or **Welcome Seafood Restaurant**, where you can sample some of Borneo's freshest seafood dishes.

Evening:
Gear up for an early start tomorrow as you begin your adventure. Overnight in Kota Kinabalu.

Day 2-3: Mount Kinabalu – The Ultimate Trek

Morning (Day 2):
Early morning transfer to **Kinabalu Park**, a UNESCO World Heritage Site. Begin your **Mount Kinabalu trek**, one of Southeast Asia's most famous mountain climbs. The trek to the summit is challenging, but the rewards of panoramic views at the top are unmatched. Hike through lush montane forests, encountering unique flora and fauna along the way.

Afternoon (Day 2):
Arrive at **Laban Rata**, the midway point, where you'll rest and prepare for the final ascent. Enjoy an overnight stay in the mountain lodge to acclimatize.

Morning (Day 3):
Wake up early to begin your **summit push** at 2-3 am for the final trek to the top of **Low's Peak** (4,095 meters). The summit rewards you with

breathtaking views of the surrounding mountains, valleys, and the **South China Sea**.

Afternoon (Day 3):
Descend back to **Kinabalu Park**, where you can relax in the cool mountain air before heading back to Kota Kinabalu. Overnight in the city.

Day 4-5: Sipadan Island – World-Class Diving

Morning (Day 4):
Fly to **Semporna**, located on the coast of Sabah, and take a boat to **Sipadan Island**, one of the world's premier dive destinations. Known for its incredible biodiversity, Sipadan offers crystal-clear waters, coral gardens, and the chance to dive with sea turtles, reef sharks, and schools of barracuda.

Afternoon (Day 4):
After arriving, you'll settle into your dive resort. **Sipadan Water Village Resort** and **Mabul Water Bungalows** are excellent accommodations for divers looking to stay close to the action. Take a first dive in the nearby waters of **Mabul Island**, famous for its macro marine life, including vibrant nudibranchs and pygmy seahorses.

Day 5:
Spend the entire day diving in **Sipadan's** incredible dive sites, such as **Barracuda Point**, **Turtle Tomb**, and **Drop Off**. If you're an experienced diver, you may even encounter large pelagic creatures like **whale sharks** and **manta rays**. Non-divers can also enjoy snorkeling and relaxing on the pristine beaches.

Evening (Day 5):
Relax and unwind in your beachfront bungalow after a long day of underwater exploration.

Day 6: Tawau Hills Park – Waterfalls and Hiking

Morning:
After breakfast, return to **Semporna** and transfer to **Tawau Hills Park**, a hidden gem known for its rainforest trails, waterfalls, and natural beauty.

Afternoon:
Embark on a trek through the park's lush trails, where you'll encounter towering trees, diverse bird species, and wildlife. **Tawau Hills Park** is home to beautiful waterfalls such as **Kinasan Waterfall**, which is ideal for a refreshing swim.

Evening:
Spend the night in the park's **eco-lodge** for a truly immersive experience in Borneo's wilderness.

Day 7: Danum Valley Conservation Area – Rainforest Adventure

Morning:
Fly back to **Kota Kinabalu** and then take a short flight to **Danum Valley**, located in the heart of Sabah's rainforest. This pristine, remote conservation area offers opportunities for adventurous jungle trekking and wildlife viewing.

Afternoon:
Arrive at your accommodation, **Borneo Rainforest Lodge**, a luxury eco-lodge nestled deep within the rainforest. Explore the lodge's surrounding trails and participate in a **guided nature walk**, where you might spot **orangutans**, **sun bears**, and **proboscis monkeys**.

Evening:
Join a **night safari** in the rainforest. This thrilling experience allows you to observe nocturnal creatures such as **slow lorises** and **civets** in their natural habitat.

Day 8: Mulu Caves – Limestone Wonders

Morning:
Fly to **Mulu National Park** in **Sarawak**, home to some of the world's largest and most impressive caves, including the famous **Sarawak Chamber**.

Afternoon:
Embark on a **cave exploration** tour, visiting **Deer Cave** (known for its nightly bat exodus) and **Lang Cave** (famous for its stalactites and stalagmites). The **Sarawak Chamber** is the largest cave chamber in the world, and exploring it is an exhilarating experience.

Evening:
Return to your accommodation in **Mulu** and enjoy a relaxing evening.

Day 9: Bako National Park – Jungle Trekking and Wildlife

Morning:
Fly to **Kuching**, the capital of **Sarawak**, and take a short boat ride to **Bako National Park**, one of Borneo's oldest and most accessible national parks. The park is a haven for trekkers, offering a variety of trails that lead to unique ecosystems.

Afternoon:
Hike through Bako's **mangrove swamps**, **tropical rainforest**, and **cliffside trails**. The park is famous for its diverse wildlife, including **proboscis monkeys** and a variety of birds and reptiles. The trek to **Telok Paku Beach** is an excellent way to experience the park's beauty.

Evening:
Return to **Kuching** for an evening of relaxation and exploration of the

city. Try local delicacies such as **Sarawak Laksa** and **Hinava** at one of the city's popular restaurants.

Day 10: Kuching – Cultural Exploration

Morning:
On your final day, take a morning trip to the **Sarawak Cultural Village**, a living museum that showcases the cultural diversity of Borneo's indigenous tribes. Explore traditional longhouses and enjoy interactive performances.

Afternoon:
Visit **Fort Margherita** for a dose of Borneo's colonial history, then head to the **Kuching Waterfront** for a leisurely walk and last-minute shopping.

Evening:
Conclude your 10-day adventure with a celebratory dinner at a waterfront restaurant, such as **The Junk** or **Top Spot Food Court**, where you can enjoy fresh seafood and reflect on your unforgettable journey through Borneo.

Adventure Seekers Tips:

- **Physical Preparation**: Many of the activities in this itinerary are physically demanding, such as the **Mount Kinabalu trek** and **diving in Sipadan**. Ensure you're in good physical condition, especially for trekking and diving activities.
- **Pack Smart**: Bring lightweight, moisture-wicking clothing for trekking, along with sturdy hiking boots and water shoes for caves and waterfalls. Don't forget a **dry bag** for your diving gear and electronics.

- **Guided Tours**: Many of the national parks and caves require a local guide. Pre-booking tours will enhance your experience and ensure safety.
- **Health and Safety**: Ensure you have the necessary vaccinations and medications for travel. Be cautious about wildlife and insects when trekking, and always follow your guide's instructions.

This **10-day adventure itinerary** offers the perfect combination of trekking, diving, and wildlife exploration. Whether you're scaling mountains, diving with marine life, or exploring dense rainforests, Borneo provides an adventure of a lifetime for those seeking thrills. Each day brings new excitement and challenges, making this journey unforgettable.

Relaxation and Wellness Itinerary (5 Days): Beaches and Rejuvenation

Borneo, with its pristine beaches, serene landscapes, and calming tropical atmosphere, is the perfect destination for those seeking rest and rejuvenation. This **5-day itinerary** is designed for travelers looking to unwind, indulge in spa treatments, and enjoy the natural beauty of Borneo's beaches and islands. With a blend of luxury resorts, wellness retreats, and calming activities, this itinerary offers a chance to relax both physically and mentally while immersing yourself in Borneo's natural wonders.

Day 1: Arrival in Kota Kinabalu, Sabah

Morning:
Arrive at **Kota Kinabalu International Airport** and transfer to your luxurious beach resort, such as **Gayana Marine Resort** or **Shangri-La's**

Tanjung Aru Resort & Spa. These resorts are known for their stunning seaside views, world-class service, and tranquil atmosphere.

Afternoon:
Unwind with a gentle stroll along the **Kota Kinabalu Waterfront** and enjoy the laid-back vibes of the city. You can relax at a café with an ocean view or indulge in a calming **spa treatment** at your resort.

Evening:
Enjoy a delicious seafood dinner at a beachside restaurant like **Welcome Seafood Restaurant**, with fresh catches prepared in traditional Bornean style. Watch the sunset as you unwind by the water.

Day 2: Explore Tunku Abdul Rahman Marine Park

Morning:
Take a short boat ride from Kota Kinabalu to **Tunku Abdul Rahman Marine Park**, a group of five idyllic islands that offer a serene environment for relaxation. **Manukan Island**, the largest island, is particularly popular for its beautiful beaches and crystal-clear waters.

Afternoon:
Spend the day soaking up the sun, swimming, or enjoying gentle snorkeling around the island's coral reefs. If you prefer, opt for a **private beach cabana** at one of the luxury resorts on the island to rest and relax. Enjoy a light, healthy lunch by the sea—perhaps a freshly made seafood salad or tropical fruit platter.

Evening:
End your day with a leisurely **sunset cruise** around the islands, offering spectacular views of the Bornean coastline. Return to your resort for a **relaxing evening at the spa**, perhaps indulging in a calming massage or a soothing body scrub.

Day 3: Spa Day and Wellness Retreat

Morning:
Treat yourself to a full **wellness experience** at one of the top resorts offering specialized spa treatments. Head to the **Mandara Spa** at **Shangri-La's Rasa Ria Resort** or the **Gayana Marine Resort Spa**, both offering a wide array of signature massages, body wraps, and holistic treatments.

Enjoy a **morning detoxification session**, such as a herbal steam bath or a traditional Bornean massage, followed by a fresh fruit smoothie or detoxifying herbal tea.

Afternoon:
Relax in the resort's peaceful surroundings, taking part in a **yoga or meditation class** to center your mind and body. Many wellness resorts in Borneo offer wellness-focused activities like guided meditation or Tai Chi in the early afternoon, perfect for those seeking inner peace.

Evening:
After your spa treatments, enjoy a light **healthy dinner** featuring organic, locally sourced ingredients. Opt for a dish with fresh seafood, vegetables, and tropical fruits, all known for their rejuvenating qualities. A soothing **foot massage** at the resort is the perfect way to end a day of self-care.

Day 4: Beach and Water Activities in Mabul Island

Morning:
Transfer to **Mabul Island**, a peaceful and quiet destination ideal for relaxation. Stay at the **Mabul Water Bungalows** or the luxurious **Sutera Harbour Resort** for an exclusive and tranquil experience. Mabul is known for its pristine beaches, clear waters, and spectacular marine life.

Afternoon:
Take a **gentle boat ride** to explore the surrounding islands, enjoy some light snorkeling, or simply relax by the beach. You can also indulge in a **traditional Malay herbal bath**, or even try a relaxing **aromatherapy massage** right on the beach, surrounded by the soothing sounds of the ocean.

Evening:
Enjoy a peaceful **sunset at the beach**, followed by a romantic dinner in a seaside restaurant. Experience the flavors of Borneo with a blend of local and international cuisine, complemented by the island's serene atmosphere.

Day 5: Departure and Final Relaxation

Morning:
On your final day, start with a **morning yoga session** or a peaceful walk along the beach to take in the sunrise. The calm atmosphere of **Mabul Island** offers the perfect opportunity for reflection and relaxation before heading home.

If you have time, visit **Sipadan Water Village Resort's spa** for a final indulgence, such as a rejuvenating facial treatment or an essential oil body massage. Let the serene surroundings enhance your experience.

Afternoon:
After a final wellness treatment, enjoy a light lunch at your resort before preparing for your departure. Spend your last few hours relaxing by the beach or taking a short stroll through the local markets for souvenirs.

Evening:
Take a final transfer to **Kota Kinabalu International Airport**, refreshed and rejuvenated, ready to return home with memories of a peaceful and fulfilling wellness retreat.

Relaxation and Wellness Tips:

- **Hydration is Key**: Tropical climates can be hot, so make sure to drink plenty of water throughout your stay.
- **Pack Light**: Bring lightweight, breathable clothing for lounging and beach activities, along with swimwear for water activities.
- **Balance Your Wellness Routine**: Take advantage of spa and wellness treatments while also making time for quiet relaxation and reflection.
- **Wellness Retreats**: Borneo has a growing number of wellness retreats that offer detox programs, yoga, and stress-relief treatments. Check with resorts for packages.

This **5-day wellness and relaxation itinerary** is designed to provide travelers with a perfect balance of serene beaches, rejuvenating spa experiences, and indulgent relaxation. Borneo's natural beauty, combined with its luxurious resorts and wellness-focused activities, makes it an ideal destination for anyone looking to recharge and refresh in a peaceful tropical paradise.

Chapter 9

Insider Tips: Local Customs and Etiquette

Borneo is a cultural mosaic, where multiple ethnic groups, traditions, and beliefs coexist harmoniously. Whether you're visiting the Malay, Dayak, Iban, or other indigenous communities, respecting local customs and etiquette will ensure a smooth and memorable experience. Here's a guide to help you navigate these cultural nuances and immerse yourself in Borneo's rich heritage with respect.

Respecting Tribal Traditions

The indigenous tribes of Borneo, such as the Dayak, Iban, and Kadazan-Dusun, have a deep connection with their land and traditions. Their customs are an integral part of the Bornean identity and should be approached with reverence.

- **Greeting Traditions**: When visiting Dayak or Iban villages, a common greeting is the handshake, but it is often softer than the western grip. In some cases, a **gesture of respect**, such as bowing slightly, may be preferred.

- **Respect for Elders**: In tribal communities, elders are highly revered. If you are invited into an indigenous home or community gathering, always greet the elders first and show your respect by offering a polite bow or slight nod.

- **Sacred Sites**: Some areas of cultural significance, such as **longhouses** or sacred burial grounds, should be approached with care. It's important to ask for permission before entering or taking photographs. In some communities, taking photos of specific rituals or ceremonies may be considered disrespectful.

- **Avoid Touching Sacred Objects**: Sacred artifacts or statues should not be touched or moved without permission. In places like the **Sarawak Cultural Village**, where indigenous displays and artifacts are shown, be mindful of what is considered sacred.

Dos and Don'ts: Dress Codes and Behavior

While Borneo is known for its relaxed and laid-back atmosphere, adhering to the dress codes and local behavior expectations is essential for fostering good relations with locals and respecting their culture.

- **Modesty is Key**: In general, modesty in dress is highly valued across Borneo. This is especially important when visiting religious sites like **mosques** or temples. For men and women, it's respectful to cover shoulders, avoid short skirts, and wear appropriate clothing in these sacred spaces.

- **Local Communities**: When visiting rural villages or indigenous communities, it's a good idea to dress modestly. Avoid wearing clothing that is too revealing. A simple outfit such as a t-shirt and long pants or skirts will be more respectful in these settings.

- **Footwear Etiquette**: When entering homes, places of worship, or temples, it is customary to remove shoes. This shows respect for the sacredness of the space. If you're unsure, follow the lead of the locals around you.

- **Hand Gestures**: When handing something to a local, especially to an elder, use your **right hand**. The left hand is often considered impolite or less respectful in many parts of Borneo.

- **Photographs**: Always ask for permission before taking photographs, especially of people, sacred sites, and rituals. While locals may be more than happy to pose for photos, it's courteous to request permission first.

Negotiation Tips for Markets

Markets in Borneo, from vibrant street stalls to bustling night markets, provide an exciting opportunity to interact with locals and purchase handmade goods, local crafts, and fresh produce. Knowing how to navigate market negotiations can enhance your experience and help you get the best deals while respecting the local customs.

- **Bartering is Common**: In many local markets, especially in **Kota Kinabalu** or **Kuching**, bartering is a common practice. When purchasing items like textiles, souvenirs, or handicrafts, expect to negotiate the price. However, keep in mind that prices are usually already reasonable for tourists, so ensure your bargaining doesn't feel too aggressive.

- **Start Low, But Be Fair**: While it's customary to offer a lower price than the initial asking price, aim to negotiate in a respectful manner. Starting at about **half the asking price** is a typical starting point, but be ready to settle at a reasonable middle ground.

- **Smile and Be Friendly**: A warm smile and friendly attitude will go a long way. Locals value friendly interaction, and being courteous and respectful during negotiations will often help lower prices. Conversely, getting too aggressive or rude will usually drive up the price.

- **Don't Rush**: Negotiation in Borneo is often about building rapport. Engage in some casual conversation about the item you're interested in, and don't be in a hurry to close the deal. The process is often just as enjoyable for the seller as it is for the buyer.

- **Respect Local Products**: If you're purchasing traditional items like **handwoven baskets**, **wooden crafts**, or **batik fabrics**, show genuine interest and respect for the craftsmanship. Complimenting the quality of the goods before negotiating shows that you value their work, and can make the process smoother.

Etiquette for Dining

Dining etiquette in Borneo varies slightly across different ethnic groups, but there are some general guidelines to keep in mind to ensure that your behavior is respectful and appreciated.

- **Use Both Hands**: When handing food to someone, use both your right and left hand, as this is a sign of respect, particularly in more traditional or indigenous communities.

- **Rice and Local Delicacies**: Rice plays a central role in Bornean meals. In the more rural areas, meals may be eaten **with your hands**, especially if you're enjoying dishes like **nasi lemak** or **lemang** (sticky rice wrapped in bamboo). Always wash your hands before eating in this case, and remember to eat with your right hand.

- **Be Polite**: If you're invited to someone's home, it is customary to accept a small portion of everything offered to you, even if you aren't hungry. This is seen as a sign of respect and appreciation for the host's hospitality.

- **Refusing Food**: If you don't wish to eat something, it's polite to gently refuse, but you should try to avoid saying "no" too directly. A softer refusal like "I am full" or "I am not able to eat that" is typically more acceptable.

Quick Reference: Key Dos and Don'ts

Do:

- Be respectful and polite with all interactions.
- Ask permission before taking photographs, especially of people and sacred sites.
- Be patient and friendly when negotiating prices at local markets.
- Wear modest clothing in religious and cultural spaces.
- Use your right hand when handing or receiving items from others.

Don't:

- Enter homes or sacred sites without first removing your shoes.
- Touch sacred objects without permission.
- Bargain aggressively or rudely in local markets.
- Point with your finger at people or objects—use your whole hand or the thumb instead.
- Engage in loud or disruptive behavior in public places.

Understanding and respecting these local customs, dress codes, and negotiation tips will enrich your Bornean experience and ensure your interactions with locals are both respectful and meaningful. Embrace the beauty of cultural exchange, and let your Bornean adventure be both enriching and respectful of its diverse traditions.

Chapter 10

Shopping and Souvenirs

Borneo is a treasure trove of unique, hand-crafted goods and authentic local products. Whether you're exploring bustling markets or visiting artisan workshops, the island offers an array of souvenirs that reflect its rich cultural diversity and natural bounty. However, when shopping in Borneo, it's essential to approach purchases with an eye for quality and ethical sourcing, ensuring your souvenirs support local artisans and sustainable practices.

Handmade Crafts and Beadwork

Borneo is famous for its **intricate beadwork** and **handmade crafts**, each piece representing the region's rich indigenous heritage. These items not only make for wonderful souvenirs but also serve as a meaningful connection to the island's traditions and craftsmanship.

- **Beadwork**: Among the most iconic crafts of Borneo are the **Iban and Dayak** beadworks, which have been passed down through generations. These vibrant and detailed beaded accessories are often used in traditional attire, ceremonies, and celebrations. **Necklaces, bracelets**, and **earrings** crafted with tiny beads in geometric patterns are common, each design signifying a specific cultural meaning. **Kain Samping**, a beaded belt worn by Iban men during ceremonial events, is also a popular collectible.

- **Weaving and Textiles**: The Dayak people of Sarawak are also known for their beautiful **handwoven textiles**, including the **ikat** fabric, which features vibrant patterns and colors. These textiles are typically made from natural fibers, including cotton, silk, and bamboo, and can be found in various forms, such as **shawls,**

scarves, bags, and **clothing**. **Songket**, another type of traditional woven fabric, is often made with gold or silver threads and is perfect for special occasions.

- **Wood Carvings**: Traditional **wood carvings**, often produced by indigenous artisans, are another significant part of Borneo's craft culture. The carvings may include **masks, figurines**, or **animals**, and are usually made from local woods like **ironwood** or **rattan**. These items are not only decorative but also carry spiritual significance, especially in Iban and Dayak culture.

- **Beaded Hats and Headdresses**: Traditionally worn during ceremonies and celebrations, these elaborately **beaded hats** or **headdresses** are now popular as keepsakes. You can find them in markets across Borneo, particularly in **Kota Kinabalu** or **Kuching**, where the indigenous cultures continue to showcase their elaborate traditional attire.

Sarawak Pepper and Sabah Tea

Borneo is known for its fertile soil and rich agricultural heritage, making it a prime location for unique culinary products that you can bring home to remember your travels.

- **Sarawak Pepper**: One of the island's most coveted agricultural products is **Sarawak Pepper**. Cultivated in the foothills of Mount Santubong, Sarawak's pepper is known for its distinct, bold flavor and is prized by chefs worldwide. Available in both **black** and **white** varieties, Sarawak Pepper is perfect for adding spice and depth to any dish. You can buy it directly from local markets or from **pepper farms** in the Sarawak region, where you can learn about the cultivation process.

- **Sabah Tea**: Known for its aromatic and rich flavor, **Sabah Tea** is grown in the lush highlands of Sabah, particularly in the **Kinabalu region**. The tea is cultivated without the use of pesticides, offering a fresh and organic experience. You can purchase it in loose-leaf or bagged forms, and it's available in **green**, **black**, and **herbal** varieties. It's a perfect souvenir for tea lovers and those looking to enjoy a piece of Borneo's pristine environment in a cup. Visit the **Sabah Tea Garden** for an authentic experience of tea tasting and to purchase tea directly from the source.

Tips for Ethical Souvenir Shopping

While shopping in Borneo, it's crucial to support ethical businesses and ensure that your purchases benefit local communities and the environment. Here are some tips to guide your shopping choices:

- **Support Local Artisans**: Choose items that are locally made, supporting artisans and small businesses. Look for handmade items that reflect the island's cultural heritage and have been crafted with care. This ensures that your money goes directly to local families and communities, rather than large commercial enterprises that may exploit workers.

- **Check for Certifications**: For products like **Sabah Tea** or **Sarawak Pepper**, check for organic or fair-trade certifications, ensuring that the products are sustainably sourced and grown. Some markets and stores offer information about the farmers and ethical practices behind their goods.

- **Avoid Endangered Species Products**: Never purchase items made from endangered wildlife, such as **ivory**, **turtle shells**, or **tiger parts**. Borneo has some of the world's most unique and endangered species, and buying such items fuels illegal trade and threatens biodiversity. Instead, opt for wildlife-inspired crafts, such as **wooden carvings** or **paintings** of local animals.

- **Opt for Sustainable Products**: When purchasing souvenirs made from natural materials, such as **wood**, **rattan**, or **bamboo**, ensure that they come from sustainable sources. Look for products that are created without the use of harmful chemicals, and avoid items that could contribute to deforestation or environmental degradation.

- **Negotiate Fairly**: While haggling is a part of the market experience in Borneo, always be fair and respectful when negotiating. Keep in mind that artisans rely on their sales to support their families and communities. Strive for a reasonable price that reflects the true value of the craftsmanship involved.

- **Avoid Mass-Produced Souvenirs**: Mass-produced souvenirs sold in tourist-heavy areas may be inexpensive, but they often lack authenticity and may not benefit local communities. Seek out **artisan markets** or **local workshops**, where you can find genuine, handmade goods that showcase the true spirit of Borneo.

By purchasing souvenirs that are crafted with care and attention to detail, you not only take home unique reminders of your time in Borneo but also support the island's cultural traditions and local economies. Whether you're drawn to the colorful beadwork of the Dayak people or the rich flavors of Sarawak pepper, your purchases will help preserve Borneo's beauty and heritage for generations to come.

Chapter 11

Practical Information

Before you embark on your Borneo adventure, it's essential to have a solid understanding of practical details that will make your trip easier and more enjoyable. From emergency contacts to frequently asked questions, this section covers everything you need to know for a smooth travel experience.

FAQs for Travelers

1. Do I need a visa to visit Borneo?

- **Malaysia**: If you're traveling to the Malaysian part of Borneo (Sabah and Sarawak), most nationalities can obtain a **Visa on Arrival** for stays up to 90 days, or you may be eligible for **visa-free entry** depending on your nationality. However, be sure to check with the nearest Malaysian embassy for the most up-to-date visa requirements.
- **Brunei**: Travelers visiting **Brunei** need to check if their nationality requires a visa. Many nationalities are allowed visa-free entry for stays of up to 90 days.
- **Indonesia**: For the Indonesian portion of Borneo (Kalimantan), many visitors can get a **Visa on Arrival** for up to 30 days, which can be extended. However, double-check the latest visa rules before traveling.

2. What's the best time to visit Borneo?

- The best time to visit Borneo is typically between **March and October**, during the dry season. However, you can still visit year-round, but be prepared for occasional rain during the

monsoon season (November to February), especially on the east coast of Sabah and Sarawak.

3. Is Borneo safe for travelers?

- Yes, Borneo is generally safe for travelers. Like anywhere, practice common-sense safety measures such as safeguarding your valuables, avoiding poorly lit areas at night, and respecting local customs. Ensure you use reputable guides when venturing into remote areas.

4. What vaccinations are recommended before traveling to Borneo?

- It's advisable to consult a healthcare provider before traveling for vaccinations and health advice specific to your needs. Common recommended vaccinations include **hepatitis A and B**, **typhoid**, **yellow fever**, and **malaria** prevention (depending on the area).

5. How do I get around Borneo?

- Borneo has several transport options depending on your destination:
  - **Domestic Flights**: For long distances (e.g., between Kota Kinabalu, Kuching, and Bandar Seri Begawan), flying is the most practical.
  - **Boats**: For islands or rivers, boats are the most efficient way to get around.
  - **Car Rental**: For exploring at your own pace, renting a car is popular, but be prepared for winding, rural roads in some areas.

6. Can I drink the tap water in Borneo?

- In most urban areas, tap water is **safe to drink**, but in rural areas or remote parts of Borneo, it's best to drink bottled water. Always check with local guides or accommodation staff for water safety.

7. What currency is used in Borneo?

- **Malaysia**: The currency in Borneo's Malaysian states (Sabah and Sarawak) is the **Malaysian Ringgit (MYR)**.
- **Brunei**: The **Brunei Dollar (BND)** is used.
- **Indonesia**: In Kalimantan, the **Indonesian Rupiah (IDR)** is the currency.

8. What is the best way to exchange money in Borneo?

- You can exchange money at **banks**, **currency exchange counters**, or **ATMs** in major cities and towns. Avoid exchanging money at airports, as the rates may be less favorable. Credit and debit cards are widely accepted in urban areas, but it's advisable to carry cash for smaller towns or rural destinations.

Emergency Contacts and Local Resources

Having the right emergency contacts and local resources is crucial to staying safe and well-prepared during your trip to Borneo.

Emergency Numbers:

- **Malaysia**:
  - **Police**: 999
  - **Ambulance**: 999
  - **Fire Department**: 994
  - **Tourism Helpline**: +60 3 8891 8000
- **Brunei**:
  - **Police**: 993
  - **Ambulance**: 991
  - **Fire Department**: 995
- **Indonesia (Kalimantan)**:
  - **Police**: 110
  - **Ambulance**: 118

    o **Fire Department**: 113

Local Healthcare and Hospitals:

- **Kota Kinabalu, Sabah**:
  - **Queen Elizabeth Hospital**: +60 88 240 221
  - **Kota Kinabalu Specialist Medical Centre**: +60 88 521 833
- **Kuching, Sarawak**:
  - **Sarawak General Hospital**: +60 82 276 122
  - **Kuching Specialist Medical Centre**: +60 82 232 366
- **Bandar Seri Begawan, Brunei**:
  - **Raja Isteri Pengiran Anak Saleha Hospital**: +673 224 2424
- **Banjarmasin, Kalimantan (Indonesia)**:
  - **RSUD Ulin Banjarmasin**: +62 511 336 8833

Tourist Information Centers:

- **Tourism Malaysia (Sabah)**: +60 88 212 121
- **Sarawak Tourism Board**: +60 82 423 600
- **Brunei Tourism**: +673 223 1919
- **Indonesia Tourism**: +62 21 383 8001

Useful Travel Apps:

- **Grab**: The popular ride-hailing app is available across Borneo, including cities like Kota Kinabalu, Kuching, and Bandar Seri Begawan.
- **Waze**: A reliable app for navigation in Borneo's cities and rural areas.
- **Borneo Map**: A great resource for hiking trails, national parks, and local attractions.
- **MySejahtera**: The official app for health and COVID-related updates (Malaysia).

This section of your travel guide ensures that you have everything you need for a stress-free experience in Borneo. By being informed about the common questions, emergency contacts, and resources available, you can focus on the wonders of the island and make the most of your adventure.

Chapter 12

Sustainability in Borneo Tourism

Borneo is a region that boasts unparalleled biodiversity, stunning rainforests, and rich cultural heritage. As tourism in Borneo continues to grow, so does the responsibility to protect and preserve this unique environment and the communities that call it home. Sustainable tourism is key to ensuring that future generations can enjoy the natural and cultural treasures Borneo has to offer. Below are ways you can support eco-friendly practices while traveling, as well as tips for responsible wildlife interactions.

Supporting Eco-Friendly Practices

1. Stay at Eco-Lodges and Green Hotels

- Choose accommodations that prioritize sustainability. Many eco-lodges and hotels in Borneo adopt practices that minimize their environmental impact. They focus on **energy conservation**, **waste reduction**, and **water management** while supporting local communities and wildlife conservation efforts. Look for properties with eco-certifications such as **Green Key** or **EarthCheck**.
    - **Example**: The **Danum Valley Field Centre** in Sabah is an eco-lodge that combines research and conservation efforts, allowing guests to explore the rainforest while supporting local biodiversity projects.

2. Minimize Plastic Use

- Borneo, like many parts of the world, faces challenges with plastic waste, especially in remote areas. Always carry a **reusable water bottle** and **shopping bags** to minimize plastic usage. When purchasing bottled water, opt for those in glass bottles or those that have minimal plastic packaging.

- ○ **Pro Tip**: Many eco-lodges and hotels provide refill stations for water, so you can easily top off your bottle without buying new ones.

3. Support Local and Sustainable Businesses

- When shopping, eating, or participating in activities, choose local businesses that **prioritize sustainability**. Purchase handicrafts and souvenirs made from natural or recycled materials, and avoid products made from endangered species (such as turtle shells or exotic woods).
  - ○ **Sarawak Pepper and Sabah Tea** are excellent sustainable souvenirs. These locally grown products support Borneo's agriculture industry and offer a tangible connection to the island's culture.

4. Opt for Eco-Tours and Conservation Efforts

- Opt for eco-tours and wildlife experiences led by certified guides who follow sustainable practices. These tours often include education on the environment and local wildlife, while providing financial support for **conservation** and **community initiatives**. By choosing these tours, you contribute to the protection of endangered species and the conservation of Borneo's rainforests.
  - ○ **Example**: The **Kinabatangan River Safari** offers wildlife tours that support the preservation of the river's unique ecosystem, home to species such as pygmy elephants and orangutans.

5. Respect Natural Spaces

- When exploring Borneo's natural wonders, always follow the **Leave No Trace** principles. Avoid disturbing wildlife, picking plants, or leaving behind trash. Stay on designated trails when hiking and do not venture into protected areas without a guide.

    ○   **Example**: **Gunung Mulu National Park** and **Danum Valley Conservation Area** are UNESCO World Heritage sites where responsible tourism helps ensure their preservation for generations to come.

Responsible Wildlife Interactions

Borneo is a haven for endangered species, including the **orangutan, proboscis monkeys,** and **Bornean pygmy elephants**. While visiting Borneo's wildlife parks and reserves is a remarkable experience, it's vital to engage in wildlife interactions that are respectful, ethical, and promote conservation.

1. Support Rehabilitation and Conservation Centers

- Visiting wildlife rehabilitation centers and supporting their conservation efforts is one of the most responsible ways to interact with Borneo's wildlife. For example, the **Sepilok Orangutan Rehabilitation Centre** in Sabah and the **Borneo Sun Bear Conservation Centre** are dedicated to rescuing and rehabilitating injured or orphaned animals. The entry fees support their operations and allow guests to learn about their vital work.
  - ○ **Pro Tip**: Always respect the guidelines set by these centers. Keep a safe distance from animals and refrain from feeding or attempting to touch them.

2. Respect Animal Habitats

- When participating in activities such as river safaris, jungle trekking, or wildlife viewing, remember that you are entering the animals' natural habitats. Keep noise to a minimum, move slowly, and refrain from disturbing the animals in any way.
  - ○ **Example**: During a river safari along the **Kinabatangan River**, you may encounter various species of primates,

birds, and even elephants. Avoid loud noises or sudden movements that could startle the animals.

3. Be Cautious with Wildlife Photography

- Wildlife photography is a fantastic way to capture memories, but it should always be done with caution and respect. Never use **flash photography**, as it can harm animals' eyes and disturb their natural behaviors. Additionally, be mindful of how close you get to the animals to avoid causing them stress.
    - ○ **Pro Tip**: A long lens is ideal for photographing wildlife from a safe distance without encroaching on their space.

4. Avoid Supporting Animal Exploitation

- While many wildlife experiences in Borneo are ethical and conservation-focused, there are also exploitative tours that harm animals or disrupt their natural behaviors. Avoid activities that offer **elephant rides**, **captive animal shows**, or any form of animal abuse. Do your research and ensure that the companies you choose are ethical in their practices.
    - ○ **Example**: Ethical wildlife tours will never encourage direct contact with wild animals. They focus on **observational experiences** where animals are allowed to roam freely in their natural environments.

5. Educate Yourself and Others

- Education is a powerful tool in conservation. Take the time to learn about the wildlife you encounter in Borneo, the environmental challenges they face, and the steps being taken to protect them. Share this knowledge with fellow travelers to foster a culture of respect for nature and wildlife.
    - ○ **Example**: The **Rainforest Discovery Centre** in Sepilok offers educational exhibits and programs about Borneo's flora and fauna, helping visitors understand the importance of preserving these ecosystems.

As travelers in Borneo, it's our duty to protect the extraordinary ecosystems and wildlife that make the island so unique. By choosing sustainable practices, supporting ethical wildlife tourism, and respecting local communities and traditions, you can help preserve the beauty of Borneo for future generations to explore and enjoy.

Let your journey to Borneo be a positive force—one that enhances the environment, supports local economies, and promotes conservation. In doing so, you'll ensure that Borneo's natural wonders remain intact, offering a paradise for wildlife and travelers alike for years to come.

Travel Glossary

Common Phrases in Malay and Local Dialects

Understanding a few key phrases in the local languages of Borneo can make your trip more enjoyable and immersive. While Malay (also known as Bahasa Malaysia) is the official language of Borneo, each region also boasts local dialects, including Iban, Kadazandusun, and Brunei Malay, among others. Here's a guide to some of the most commonly used phrases and terms, including useful terms for navigation:

Basic Malay Phrases

- **Hello / Hi**: *Halo* or *Hai*
- **Good Morning**: *Selamat Pagi*
- **Good Evening**: *Selamat Petang*
- **Good Night**: *Selamat Malam*
- **How are you?**: *Apa Khabar?*
- **I'm Fine**: *Khabar Baik*
- **Thank You**: *Terima Kasih*
- **Please**: *Tolong*
- **Excuse Me / Sorry**: *Maaf*
- **Yes**: *Ya*
- **No**: *Tidak*
- **Goodbye**: *Selamat Tinggal* or *Jumpa Lagi*
- **Do you speak English?**: *Adakah anda boleh berbahasa Inggeris?*

Important Travel Phrases in Malay

- **Where is the bathroom?**: *Di mana tandas?*
- **How much does this cost?**: *Berapa harga ini?*
- **I need help**: *Saya perlukan bantuan*
- **Where is…?**: *Di mana…?*
  - Example: *Di mana stesen bas?* (Where is the bus station?)

- **Can you show me?**: *Bolehkah anda tunjukkan saya?*
- **I don't understand**: *Saya tidak faham*
- **Can you repeat that?**: *Boleh anda ulangi?*
- **Where can I buy…?**: *Di mana saya boleh beli…?*
  - Example: *Di mana saya boleh beli tiket?* (Where can I buy tickets?)
- **I am lost**: *Saya sesat*
- **Help!**: *Tolong!*
- **Call the police!**: *Panggil polis!*

Useful Terms for Navigation

- **Left**: *Kiri*
- **Right**: *Kanan*
- **Straight**: *Lurus*
- **Near**: *Dekat*
- **Far**: *Jauh*
- **Turn Left**: *Pusing kiri*
- **Turn Right**: *Pusing kanan*
- **How far is it?**: *Berapa jauh?*
- **Bus Station**: *Stesen Bas*
- **Train Station**: *Stesen Kereta Api*
- **Airport**: *Lapangan Terbang*
- **Hotel**: *Hotel* (Pronounced the same way in Malay)
- **Street**: *Jalan*
- **River**: *Sungai*
- **Beach**: *Pantai*
- **Mountain**: *Gunung*
- **Park**: *Taman*

Local Dialects and Unique Phrases

Iban (Spoken in Sarawak)

- **Hello**: *Selamat Pagi* (Good Morning)

- **How are you?**: *Apa Kabar?*
- **Thank You**: *Tuan Teken*
- **Goodbye**: *Selamat Tinggal*
- **Where is the bathroom?**: *Di mana bilik mandi?*

Kadazandusun (Spoken in Sabah)

- **Hello**: *Kumai*
- **Good Morning**: *Selamat Pagi*
- **How are you?**: *Kasi apa ka?*
- **Thank You**: *Sukot*
- **Goodbye**: *Kinundah*
- **Where is the bathroom?**: *Ko diman bilik mandi?*

Brunei Malay (Spoken in Brunei)

- **Hello**: *Helo*
- **How are you?**: *Apa Khabar?*
- **Thank You**: *Terima Kasih*
- **Goodbye**: *Selamat Tinggal*
- **Where is the bathroom?**: *Di mana tandas?*

Local Terms for Attractions and Services

- **Tourist Information Center**: *Pusat Maklumat Pelancong*
- **Souvenir Shop**: *Kedai Cenderamata*
- **Restaurant**: *Restoran*
- **Cafe**: *Kafe*
- **Market**: *Pasar*
- **Bank**: *Bank*
- **ATM**: *Mesin Pengeluaran Wang Automatik (ATM)*
- **Pharmacy**: *Farmasi*
- **Hospital**: *Hospital*
- **Police Station**: *Balai Polis*

Shopping Terms

- **How much is this?**: *Berapa harga ini?*
- **Discount**: *Diskaun*
- **Expensive**: *Mahal*
- **Cheap**: *Murah*
- **I would like to buy this**: *Saya mahu beli ini*
- **Do you have this in a different size/color?**: *Adakah anda ada ini dalam saiz/warna lain?*

Health and Emergency Phrases

- **I am sick**: *Saya sakit*
- **I need a doctor**: *Saya perlukan doktor*
- **Where is the nearest hospital?**: *Di mana hospital yang terdekat?*
- **I lost my passport**: *Saya hilang pasport saya*
- **I need to report a theft**: *Saya perlu laporkan kecurian*

While English is widely understood in tourist areas, knowing a few phrases in Malay (and local dialects) can enrich your experience in Borneo. Whether you're navigating through vibrant cities or exploring remote rainforests, these phrases will help you communicate with locals, ensuring a smoother and more enjoyable adventure. Always approach cultural exchanges with respect, and your interactions will be rewarding for both you and the people you meet. Happy travels!

Acknowledgments

The creation of *Borneo Travel Guide 2025* has been an exciting and rewarding endeavor, and I am immensely grateful to the many individuals and organizations that have contributed to making this guide both informative and engaging.

To the local communities of Borneo, thank you for opening your doors and sharing your stories, culture, and traditions. Your generosity and hospitality have been invaluable in enriching this guide, offering travelers a true and respectful insight into life on this extraordinary island.

To the experts, guides, and environmentalists working tirelessly to preserve Borneo's unique ecosystems, including the rainforests, rivers, wildlife, and cultural heritage. Your dedication to conservation has ensured that future generations can experience Borneo's beauty and diversity.

To the researchers, historians, and authors whose work on Borneo's history, biodiversity, and indigenous cultures has inspired this guide. Your invaluable contributions have allowed me to share a deeper understanding of the island's rich past and present.

To my family and friends, your unwavering support, encouragement, and patience have been essential in the completion of this project. Thank you for always being there during moments of inspiration and challenge.

Finally, **to the readers and travelers** who will embark on their own journeys to Borneo, I hope this guide serves as both a practical resource and a source of inspiration. May it lead you to uncover hidden treasures, connect with local cultures, and experience the natural wonders that make Borneo truly one of a kind.

With deepest gratitude,
Julian D. Cross,
Author of *Borneo Travel Guide 2025*

Conclusion

Borneo, with its captivating blend of natural beauty, cultural heritage, and vibrant wildlife, stands as one of the world's most intriguing and diverse destinations. From the dense rainforests and towering mountains of Sabah and Sarawak to the serene shores of Brunei, this island offers something for every kind of traveler. Whether you're an intrepid explorer, a history enthusiast, or someone seeking tranquility amidst lush landscapes, Borneo promises to leave an indelible mark on your soul.

This guide has sought to illuminate the many facets of Borneo, offering practical advice and insider tips to ensure that your journey is as seamless and enriching as possible. Through detailed itineraries, essential travel information, and expert recommendations, *Borneo Travel Guide 2025* aims to empower you to make the most of your time on this magnificent island. From scaling Mount Kinabalu, one of Southeast Asia's highest peaks, to gliding along the Kinabatangan River in search of pygmy elephants, to exploring the otherworldly Mulu Caves, each corner of Borneo beckons with promise.

At the same time, this guide emphasizes the importance of responsible and sustainable travel. Borneo is not just a destination; it is a delicate ecosystem that needs our protection. With a growing awareness of eco-friendly practices and wildlife conservation, travelers have a unique opportunity to support efforts that safeguard the island's biodiversity and indigenous cultures. Whether it's choosing an eco-lodge in the rainforest, respecting local customs, or supporting community-based initiatives, your visit can contribute positively to the island's future.

In addition to its natural wonders, Borneo's cultural heritage offers a rich, immersive experience. From the colorful traditions of the Dayak tribes to the grandeur of Brunei's royal architecture, the island's cultural landscape is as varied as its environment. Each visit to Borneo is not just a trip—it's an opportunity to learn, to connect, and to witness the resilience of communities who have thrived here for centuries.

As you embark on your journey to Borneo, remember that it is a land that rewards curiosity and respect. Whether you're wandering through the bustling streets of Kuching or the tranquil forests of Danum Valley, Borneo offers profound experiences that will enrich your life long after you return home. It is a place that encourages exploration, reflection, and, above all, wonder.

In conclusion, *Borneo Travel Guide 2025* is more than just a practical handbook; it is an invitation to discover the heart of one of the world's most captivating and diverse destinations. May it guide you through lush jungles, past ancient cultures, and to hidden gems that few have the privilege to experience. No matter where your journey takes you, Borneo will forever remain a land of mystery, beauty, and endless possibility. Embrace it, respect it, and let it transform you.

Appendix

Contact Information for Travel Agencies

Borneo offers a range of travel agencies catering to different types of travelers. Whether you're seeking an organized tour, adventure packages, or luxury travel arrangements, these agencies can help make your journey seamless and unforgettable.

1. **Borneo Eco Tours (Sabah, Malaysia)**

   - **Website**: www.borneoecotours.com
   - **Contact**: +60 88 247 101
   - **Specialty**: Eco-friendly tours, wildlife safaris, cultural experiences, and adventure trips.
   - **Email**: info@borneotours.com

2. **Sabah Travel and Tours (Sabah, Malaysia)**

   - **Website**: www.sabahtravel.com
   - **Contact**: +60 88 212 189
   - **Specialty**: Customizable tours, Mount Kinabalu climbs, diving excursions, and nature walks.
   - **Email**: tours@sabahtravel.com

3. **Sarawak Tourism Board (Sarawak, Malaysia)**

   - **Website**: www.sarawaktourism.com
   - **Contact**: +60 82 423 600
   - **Specialty**: Cultural tours, wildlife exploration, and indigenous experiences.
   - **Email**: info@sarawaktourism.com

4. **Borneo Adventure (Sabah & Sarawak, Malaysia)**

   - **Website**: www.borneo-adventure.com
   - **Contact**: +60 88 252 367

- Specialty: Trekking, adventure travel, river cruises, and tours to Mulu National Park.
- Email: info@borneoadventure.com

5. **Brunei Tourism (Brunei Darussalam)**

- **Website**: www.bruneitourism.travel
- **Contact**: +673 238 2500
- **Specialty**: Cultural and historical tours, luxury travel, and unique Brunei experiences.
- **Email**: tourism@bruneitourism.travel

Suggested Reading and Resources

To deepen your understanding of Borneo's culture, ecology, and history, the following books and resources are recommended for any traveler interested in this fascinating destination:

1. **"Borneo: A History of the Land and Its People" by Redmond O'Hanlon**

   - **Description**: A detailed account of Borneo's history, people, and environment, exploring its indigenous cultures and colonial past.
   - **Why Read**: Offers an enriching perspective for travelers seeking to understand the island's heritage and complex identity.

2. **"Borneo Rainforest: The Edge of the World" by David Attenborough**

   - **Description**: A fascinating look into the ecosystems of Borneo's rainforests and the incredible diversity of its flora and fauna.

- Why Read: Perfect for nature enthusiasts who wish to learn more about the biodiversity that makes Borneo so unique.

3. **"The Cultural and Natural Heritage of Borneo" by James C. Scott**

    - Description: An in-depth exploration of Borneo's cultural landscape, including the indigenous tribes and their deep connection with the land.
    - Why Read: Provides valuable insights into the traditions and customs of the indigenous peoples of Borneo.

4. **"Lonely Planet Borneo"**

    - Description: A comprehensive travel guide to Borneo, including detailed maps, recommendations for accommodations, attractions, and advice for traveling across Sabah, Sarawak, and Brunei.
    - Why Read: Practical and up-to-date, making it an essential companion for your Borneo journey.

5. **"The End of the River: A Journey Through Borneo" by David Lamb**

    - Description: A travel memoir that takes readers along the rivers and remote places of Borneo, offering a vivid picture of the region's wildlife and indigenous tribes.
    - Why Read: Ideal for adventure seekers and those interested in off-the-beaten-path travel experiences.

6. **Borneo Travel Blogs**

    - Example: Borneo Adventure Travel Blog
    - Description: Provides up-to-date travel tips, personal stories, and in-depth information about various attractions and destinations in Borneo.
    - Why Read: A helpful resource for current travel trends and advice from fellow travelers.

7. **Borneo Eco Tours Resources**

   o **Description**: Articles, travel itineraries, and conservation updates from a leading eco-tourism provider in Borneo.
   o **Why Read**: Ideal for travelers who want to combine their adventure with responsible tourism and environmental awareness.

By utilizing these contact resources, maps, and reading materials, you'll be well-prepared to explore Borneo in depth and gain a deeper understanding of this extraordinary destination. Whether you're hiking in the rainforest, exploring the culture, or diving into the rich history, these resources will enhance your journey across this biodiverse island.

Map

BORNEO

1. Open Camera: Launch the smartphone camera app.
2. Point at QR Code: Focus your camera on the QR code.
3. Scan: Wait for your camera to identify the QR code.
4. Access: Tap the notice to view the associated material.
5. Explore: Investigate the related information, such as maps or webpages.
6. Repeat: Repeat the method for the other QR codes in the guide.

Using QR codes is as simple as pointing, scanning, and exploring with your smartphone camera!

Printed in Great Britain
by Amazon

58735969R00097